# QuickStart

# to

# JAVASCRIPT

Forest Lin
Tulsa Community College

Scott/Jones, Inc., Publishers
P. O. Box 696
El Granada, CA 94018

Voice: (650) 726-2436
Fax: (650) 726-4693
E-mail: scotjones2@aol.com
Web: http://www.scottjonespub.com

**QuickStart to JavaScript**
Forest Lin



4 W X

ISBN 1-57676-018-9

Text Design and Composition: Forest Lin
Cover Design: Kristin Bernhisel-Osborn
Book Manufacturing: Malloy Lithographing

Scott/Jones Publishing Company

Sponsoring Editorial Group: Cathy Glenn and Richard Jones
Production Manager: Heather Bennett
Marketing & Sales: Barbara Masek, Lynne McCormick, Hazel Dunlap, and Donna Cross
Business Operations: Chuck Paetzke, Michelle Robelet, and Cathy Glenn
Publisher: Richard Jones



Additional Titles of Interest from Scott/Jones
by Forest Lin

The DOS 6 Coursebook
Visual Basic Programming
The Visual Basic 5 Coursebook
ActiveX and the Internet

# About the Author

Dr. Forest Lin is a seasoned professor and author. He has taught in various colleges for the past 30 years. He has published more than a dozen computer books. They cover WordPerfect, DOS, Lotus 1-2-3, Visual Basic, HTML, VBScript, and JavaScript. They are published by Que, Wordware, Prentice-Hall, and Scott/Jones.

# Other Internet Books by Forest Lin

## Short Course in HTML

- Overview: A brief but comprehensive coverage of HTML 4 and its implementations in Netscape Navigator 4 and Internet Explorer 4
- Accessories: 20 drill and 20 practice questions/answers at the end of each chapter; a supporting Web site with source files and interactive tutorials
- Length: 320 pages
- Published: 8/98

CHAPTERS
1. Document Formatting
2. Hyperlinks and Multimedia
3. Tables and Frames
4. Cascading Style Sheets

APPENDIX
A. Internet Overview
B. HTML Tags
C. Color Values
D. Character Set
E. Glossary
F. Form Elements
G. CSS Properties
H. Web Authoring with FrontPage Express
I. Web Authoring with Word 97

## The JavaScript Coursebook

- Overview: A mid-size, comprehensive coverage of JavaScript and Web programming; useful for people who want to go beyond HTML/Web authoring; suitable for intro to computer/Internet/Web literacy/programming
- Accessories: 20 drill and 20 practice questions/answers at the end of each chapter; a supporting Web site with source files and interactive tutorials
- Length: 450 pages
- Available: Forthcoming

CHAPTERS

1. JavaScript Basics--how to use Notepad to write scripts; elementary and essential HTML tags; JavaScript overview and examples; object concepts and terms; event handling; functions and passing arguments

2. Programming Basics--language mechanics; operators; control structures

3. Form Elements--form elements (controls) and their methods, properties, and event handlers; using these elements to create interactive Web pages

4. Windows, Frames, and Documents--DOM issues; various objects and their methods, properties, and event handlers

5. Numbers and Strings--manipulating string and numeric data types by using built-in functions and objects

6. Dates, Arrays, and Custom Objects--handling date-related items, user-created arrays and objects

The book stresses the features that are common in both Netscape Navigator 4 and Internet Explorer 4. The incompatible features are only mentioned in passing. As a result, all the script examples will run in both browsers.

APPENDIX

A. Internet Overview
B. HTML Tags
C. Color Values
D. Character Set
E. Glossary
F. Computer Math
(binary, octal, hex)
G. Operators
H. Control Structures
I. Reserved Words
J. Built-In Objects and Functions
(Alphabetic listing, annotated)

## The VBScript Coursebook

- Similar to *The JavaScript Coursebook*
- Available: Forthcoming

## QuickStart to VBScript

- An abbreviated version of *The VBScript Coursebook*
- Similar to *QuickStart to JavaScript*
- Available: Forthcoming

JavaScript * QuickStart

# Table of Contents

# Preface

JavaScript is a simple and popular language to handle the Web. You can use it to learn elementary computer programming concepts and techniques. If you get good at it, you can use it to make the Web do lots of fancy and useful things.

This little book is intended for three types of people:

- Complete Novices: Those who are new to HTML and computer programming but want to learn programming in the Web/Internet environment.

- Web Sophisticates: Nonprogrammers who want to go beyond HTML/Web authoring in order to create dynamic Web pages.

- Seasoned Programmers: Those who already know programming but want to break into Web programming.

You need no knowledge of HTML or computer programming to use this book. The book will introduce you to both.

But if you have knowledge of one or both of these subjects, your job will become easier. Those who already know HTML can concentrate on programming. Those who already know programming can concentrate on the syntax of JavaScript and how to use it to manipulate HTML.

What tools do you need to break into this field? A text editor and a Web browser. In this book, we use Notepad, which comes with Windows; you can use any editor you want. The browser can be Netscape Navigator 2 or later or Internet Explorer 3 or later. If you use one of the 4.0 or later browsers, you can take advantage of more features. These browsers either come with new computers or can be downloaded from the Internet.

This book covers most of the JavaScript topics. It gives you lots of breadth but little depth. You get a taste of what these features can do. If you want more depth, you are welcome to try *The JavaScript Coursebook* by this author.

This book has four chapters. Each comes with 10 Drill and 10 Practice questions at the end. The former drill you on some simple terms and concepts. The latter require you to do something. The answers appear after the questions.

A Web site is maintained for your convenience. It stores some lengthier source files which you can download to your local drive or run right from this site to see the result. If a source code listing in the book shows a file name at the beginning, that file is available from this site.

This site also contains interactive tutorials, one for each chapter. The 10 Drill questions are driven by a CAI engine written in JavaScript. It will display each question and prompt you for an answer. If you supply a wrong answer, it will tell you why.

If your PC is connected to the Internet, the following address will take you to this site:

http://www.geocities/SiliconValley/Lab/7590/flin.html

JavaScript * QuickStart

# <1> JavaScript Basics

This chapter gets you started on writing scripts. It also provides a brief coverage of the major JavaScript features.

## JavaScript Overview

JavaScript is a computer language that handles scripts (programs) embedded in Web pages.

This language comes in the form of a separate computer program that is included with a Web browser (Netscape Navigator 2.0 or higher and Internet Explorer 3.0 or higher). This program is a language engine that interprets scripts and acts on them. So JavaScript is often called an interpreted language. Each browser comes with its own JavaScript interpreter (a dynamic-link library file that has the .dll extension).

A JavaScript programmer can embed a script (program code written in ASCII text) in a Web page. When a browser encounters the script, it will call its .dll file to interpret (parse) and act on the script. The script can thus make the Web page active and dynamic.

An **interpreted language** is different from a **compiled language**. The latter can convert program source code into a machine-readable binary format, which can then run by itself. An interpreted language reads program code on the fly and performs action accordingly. A JavaScript script is an interpreted program which can be executed by JavaScript the interpreter; it cannot run outside of the interpreter.

JavaScript was invented by Netscape to make its browser more useful. It was modeled after C, C++, and Java. All these languages follow similar syntactical rules. JavaScript is obviously the simplest of them. It is thus suitable for beginners to break into computer programming. It is also useful for Web-savvy people who want to liven up their Web sites. So, as the Web and Netscape Navigator became wildly popular, JavaScript quickly became a widely used tool.

As Microsoft entered the Web browser battle, it had to offer a compatible tool so that Internet Explorer (Microsoft's Web browser) could handle all the Web pages with embedded scripts. Its offering is known as **JScript**. With some minor exceptions, it's mostly compatible with Netscape's JavaScript. So your scripts should have few problems with either browser. (Microsoft also offers **VBScript**, which can be handled by Internet Explorer; but Netscape Navigator requires a plug-in to process it.)

A Web browser processes **HTML tags** (commands used to create Web pages) and displays the results in a Web page. That was all the old browsers could do. New browsers will also do the same thing if no script is involved. If scripts are involved, they can take over after the browser finishes its parsing job. The scripts can now interact with the user who might want to do something to the objects created by the HTML tags.

JavaScript is a language that enables the user to do something to the Web objects created by HTML tags. Suppose the user clicks a button created by an HTML tag. Some action is supposed to happen. This is where the programmer comes in. You the programmer are supposed to write a script that will make the action happen.

JavaScript programmers need to face two fronts: the Web and the language. They need to:

- Know a fair amount of HTML tags.
- Master JavaScript's language mechanics and built-in objects and functions.
- Combine the above two to make a Web site lively and useful.

This book is devoted primarily to JavaScript and secondarily to HTML. (Another book by this author covers HTML.) It will be helpful if you have some knowledge of HTML. If not, the "HTML Basics" section below will get you started.

# Using A Text Editor

A Web page contains nothing but pure ASCII (American Standard Code for Information Interchange) text, which does not contain formatting characters common in word processors. When you embed HTML tags (enclosed between < and >), a browser parses (interprets) them and displays the results for viewers. Scripts are also

ASCII text embedded in the Web page and mixed together with HTML tags. A Web author and script programmer need to use a text editor to enter the text.

Any text editor that can save ASCII files will work, so you are free to use your favorite editor. If you use a word processor, make sure you save the text in the ASCII format.

To author a Web page and embed a script in that page, you need to follow these general steps:

- Use a text editor to create a file with the .htm or .html extension.
- Use a Web browser to load the above file.
- Go to the editor to make revisions and resave the file.
- Go to the browser and reload the same file to see the new result.

If you have no preference in a text editor, **Notepad** is a good start. It comes with all PCs because it's part of the Windows package. To run Notepad, choose Start | Programs | Accessories | Notepad. An empty window is ready for you to type something. After that, you can save your file by choosing File | Save (or Save As) and supply a file name and, if necessary, a directory path. Make sure the file extension (after the dot) is .htm or .html.

You are now ready to display your file in a browser. Run the browser of your choice. This can be done by double-clicking an appropriate icon on your desktop or choosing Start | Programs | Netscape Navigator or Internet Explorer. In the Address field at the top of the browser window, enter the file name and its path, such as:

```
a:\myfile.html
```

That will load a specified file from drive A's root directory (assuming your file is saved there). The browser now displays your file's contents. If you want to revise your file, go to Notepad and make changes. Then save the new version over the old. Then go to the browser window and refresh the file. You can press F5 in Internet Explorer or Ctrl+R in Netscape Navigator to reload the file from disk. The new version now appears.

# HTML Basics

A Web page contains **HTML tags** in order to mark up text to display in specific fonts, sizes, colors, etc. Here is the bare minimum:

```
<HTML>
<BODY>
Page content goes here.
</BODY>
</HTML>
```

Suppose you type the above lines in Notepad and save it to an .html file. Loading it to a browser will show the single text line. The tags are not shown; they control the content instead.

HTML tags usually come in pairs. The start tag, such as <BODY> is terminated by a matching end tag, which has an additional / sign (</BODY>). Tags can be typed in any case you wish. So browsers will treat <body>, <Body>, and <BODY> as equivalent.

If you want to add text to your browser's title bar, use the <TITLE> tag placed in the <HEAD> tag. The following example will lead to Figure 1.1.

```
<HTML>
<HEAD>
<TITLE>My Page</TITLE>
</HEAD>
<BODY>
This is the body text of my page.
<!--This comment line is not shown.-->
</BODY>
</HTML>
```

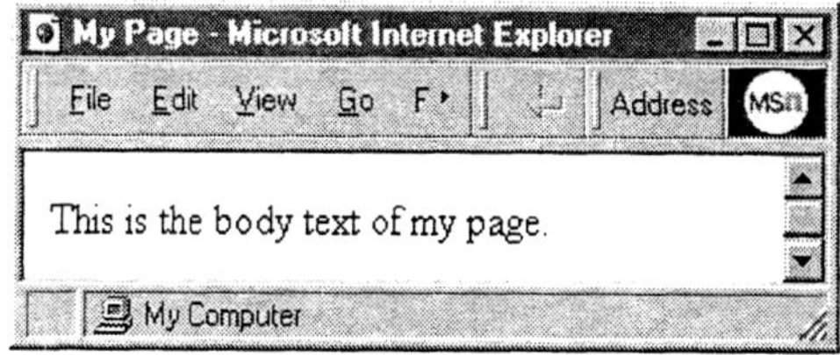


**Figure 1.1 A Web page with title and body**

Our source code also includes a **comment**. It's placed between <!-- and -->. Anything appearing inside the pair is ignored by a browser.

A Web page's text and tags can be in any shape you want. In our example, we could have lumped all the separate lines into a single continuous line (by taking away all the carriage returns), and the result (output display) would not change. However, by arranging the source document in a logical manner, you enhance readability and can more easily modify and debug errant tags.

Some codes that a text processor can act on are ignored by browsers. They include tabs, carriage returns, and extra spaces (horizontal or vertical). A two-line text separated by a hard return will be displayed in one line, with a space separating the two. Tabs and multiple spaces will be replaced by one space.

Browsers manage text flow by wrapping long text lines and supplying scroll bars when necessary. As you change the size of the browser window, the text inside may change shape. If you want to control text flow or display some unusual characters, you need to use tags or special codes.

The following basic tags should be enough to get you started. Each requires a matching end tag, unless otherwise noted.

| | |
|---|---|
| <B> | Bolded text. |
| <BR> | Inserts a line break; no end tag. |
| <CENTER> | To horizontally center a block of text. |
| <FONT> | Used with COLOR to specify a text color and SIZE to specify a size from 1 (smallest) to 7 (largest). |
| <H1> | Large and bolded text; <H6> is smallest. |
| <HR> | Inserts a horizontal rule (line); no end tag. |
| <I> | Italic text. |
| <P> | Inserts a paragraph break; end tag optional. |
| <PRE> | Preformatted text, using a monospaced font and maintaining the original text conditions such as tabs and breaks. |
| <SUB> | Subscript. |
| <SUP> | Superscript. |

If you want to insert a break, use <BR> or <P>. The latter adds a vertical space that is about one and half times that of the former. Multiple <BR> tags add multiple breaks, but multiple <P> tags will add only one paragraph break.

The following two examples will produce the same result:

```
line 1<BR>line 2

line 1<BR>
line 2
```

Both will produce two lines. So your source file's shape does not affect the output display. The tags do that.

The <PRE> tag is used to display text in a **monospaced font**, which, in contrast to a **proportional font**, displays each character in the same amount of horizontal space. Furthermore, tabs, extra spaces, and line breaks will all be preserved.

Consider this example:

```
<PRE>one          two
three
four</PRE>
```

Three lines will appear, and the gap in the first line will also be kept. If you take away the <PRE> tag, the text will merge into a single line without additional spaces.

To display headings, use <H1> for the first level, <H2> for the second level, and so on. These are **block-level tags** because they automatically insert a break before and after the text.

The following will produce two lines, with the first larger than the second:

```
<H1>Heading One</H1>
<H2>Heading Two</H2>
```

Some tags are **text-level** because they don't insert breaks. Some tags also come with **attributes** that let you assign various values. The <FONT> tag is a good example. Consider the following example:

```
regular text <FONT SIZE=7>large</FONT>
<FONT SIZE=2 COLOR="red"> small red</FONT>
```

The above will produce a single line because <FONT> does not add breaks. The size of the middle word will be much larger. And the last two words will also be red.

In assigning a value to an attribute, you can use any case or optionally enclose a value in quotes. Many tags come with multiple values. You need to consult a book or some online source if you intend to use these tags.

Future sections will encounter more tags as we use scripts to manipulate them. They will be explained when the time comes.

# Static and Dynamic Pages

When you visit a Web site, you are downloading a Web page to your browser. The page may contain text and graphics. You may look at them and click another link to download another page. These are **static pages** because they don't do anything other than presenting information.

On the other hand, you may have encountered some sites where you register for something or order some merchandise like a book or a plane ticket. You may be asked to fill out a form by entering your name or credit card number in some text boxes, to make some selections in checkboxes or radio buttons, and to click a Submit button. Upon clicking, you may get a message telling you that you forgot to fill in the required information in a text box. After you complete everything as required and click Submit, you may get a message telling you to expect your book or ticket in a week.

Here you are encountering a **dynamic page**. Such a page usually involves forms and scripts. Forms contain visual objects like text boxes and command (push) buttons. Scripts are programs to manipulate those objects. A Web programmer needs to use both to create a dynamic page to interact with users.

A form is created with the <FORM> tag. An area between the start and end tags becomes a form. A Web page may contain multiple forms.

The visual objects inside a form are commonly called **form elements**, **form objects**, **form controls** (or just controls for short). They are also called **input fields** because they are created mostly with the <INPUT> tag and users are required to enter input information in them. Chapter 3 provides more details about these objects.

As a demonstration, type in Notepad the following source file exactly as shown and then load it to your browser:

```
<HTML>
<HEAD>
<TITLE>Form Demo</TITLE>
</HEAD>
<BODY>
<H3>Welcome to my page.</H3>
<FORM NAME="form1">
<INPUT TYPE="text" NAME="txtName">
</FORM>
<SCRIPT LANGUAGE="JavaScript">
<!--
```

```
  name1 = prompt("Enter your first name:", "")
  document.form1.txtName.value = "Hi, " + name1
//-->
</SCRIPT>
It's good to see you.
</BODY>
</HTML>
```

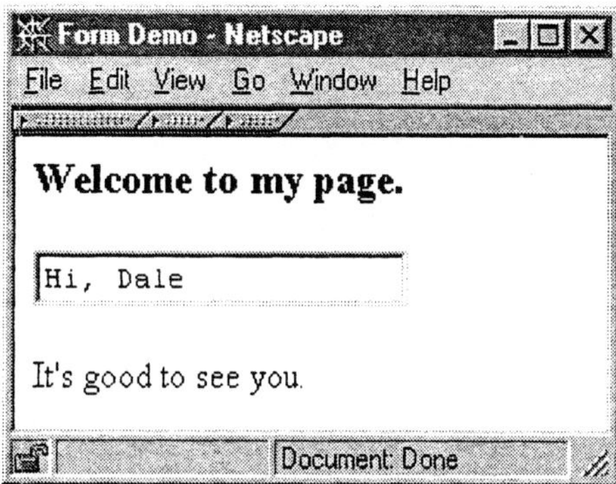


**Figure 1.2 An interactive page**

The source file will produce Figure 1.2. The browser will behave as follows:

1. Display the <H3> text line.

2. Create a text box.

3. Show a prompt box to prompt you to enter your name.

4. Enter your name into the text box.

5. Display the last line.

The text you enter in the prompt box (see another section below) is assigned to a variable named **`name1`**. This string will then be combined with "Hi" and entered into the text box.

You may understand the source code better in later sections. For now, we're going to use this example to illustrate OOP, discussed in the next section.

# Object Concepts and Terms

You may have noticed the weird statement like this:

```
document.form1.txtName.value = "Hi, " + name1
```

Here we are assigning a value to a property that is an object which in turn belongs to another object. A little knowledge of objects will help.

An **object** is simply a computer program that is packaged as a distinct unit with certain characteristics. To make it easier for programmers to handle complex situations, program code is packaged into an object. Various related objects are tied together in a hierarchical order. So an object may be a child of another object, which may the parent of multiple children.

JavaScript is an object-based language, which follows the conventions in object-oriented programming (OOP). Such a language involves using commands to manipulate objects.

Let's use a car as an example. It possesses certain attributes and can perform some actions. In OOP, the former are known as **properties** and the latter as **methods**. Properties may include the car's weight, color, price tag, etc. Methods may include actions like starting, driving, braking, parking, etc. Properties and methods are also collectively known as the **members** of the object. An object may also include **events** among its members.

To make it easy to refer to an object's properties and methods, OOP uses a **dot notation** by connecting the object's name and a member's name with a dot. So we may have car.color or car.weight when we want to reference properties. In **pseudocode** (English-like statements), we may say:

```
assign red to car.color
show car.color
```

In real life, this scheme is similar to using Smith.Joe, Smith.Jane, or Smith.Grandpa to identify the members of the Smith family.

We can do the same thing with methods, which are commonly named with verbs in contrast to naming properties with nouns. So we might say:

```
car.drive
car.stop
```

To be more precise when we want to do something to an object, we may want to **pass an argument** to a method like this:

```
car.drive(60)
```

Here we mean to drive the car at 60 miles per hour. By passing different values, we can make our object behave differently.

A program like a browser may have built-in objects. You can use these objects to do things for you. To use these objects, you need to find out what they are (their exact names) and what they can do (properties, methods, and events). By using an available member, you can do things such as changing the background color of a Web page. So it's important for a programmer to find out the available objects and their services.

In JavaScript, you can also create your own objects and endow them with properties and methods. You can then maneuver the objects as you do with built-in objects created by somebody else.

# JavaScript Basic Structure

To insert a script, you generally follow this pattern:

```
<HTML>
<HEAD>
<TITLE>title here</TITLE>
<SCRIPT LANGUAGE="JavaScript">
<!--
//script here
//-->
</SCRIPT>
</HEAD>
<BODY>
body and tags here
<SCRIPT LANGUAGE="JavaScript">
<!--
/*
you can also
place code here
*/
//-->
</BODY>
</HTML>
```

A script can be placed in the head and/or body of a document. The <!-- and --> tags hide the script from a browser that can't handle it. In that case, the entire script block is ignored.

Wherever you place your script, make sure to put it between the top two and bottom two lines as shown below. If anything is missing, either the script won't run or an error will greet you.

```
<SCRIPT LANGUAGE="JavaScript">
<!--
script here
//-->
</SCRIPT>
```

JavaScript comments are placed after // (single-line comment) or between /* and */. Comments are ignored by a browser. The // sign before --> is necessary because it prevents the language parser from reading -->, which is not a valid JavaScript statement.

The LANGUAGE attribute is optional. If you just use <SCRIPT> without specifying a language, both browsers will default to JavaScript.

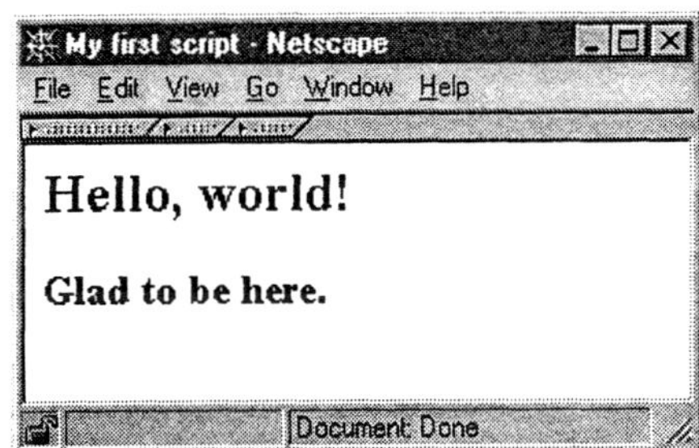


Figure 1.3 Outputting text

Here is a practical example. It produces Figure 1.3.

```
<HTML>
<HEAD>
<TITLE>My first script</TITLE>
</HEAD>
<BODY>
<SCRIPT LANGUAGE="JavaScript">
<!--
```

```
  document.write ("<H2>Hello, world!</H2>")
  document.write ("<H3>Glad to be here.</H3>")
  //this is my very first script
//-->
</SCRIPT>
</BODY>
</HTML>
```

We could have placed the following tags outside of the script block to produce the same result:

```
<H2>Hello, world!</H2>
<H3>Glad to be here.</H3>
```

Instead, we're making the script do the job. Just remember to place script statements inside a script block.

In our example, we use the **write** method of the **document** object to produce the display. Here we are writing text to the document object which is the equivalent of the <BODY> block in HTML. The common objects and their members will be covered in Chapters 3 and 4.

# Dialog Boxes

There are three **dialog boxes** that are useful for user interaction. These are known as **alert box**, **prompt box**, and **confirm box**. These are introduced here so that we can start using them.

**Figure 1.4 An alert box**

The alert box simply displays a message; it's useful when you want to tell something to the user. The following script statement will display the box shown in Figure 1.4.

```
alert("Hello, welcome to my page.")
```

The prompt box follows this syntax:

```
userAnswer = prompt("message in box", defaultEntry)
```

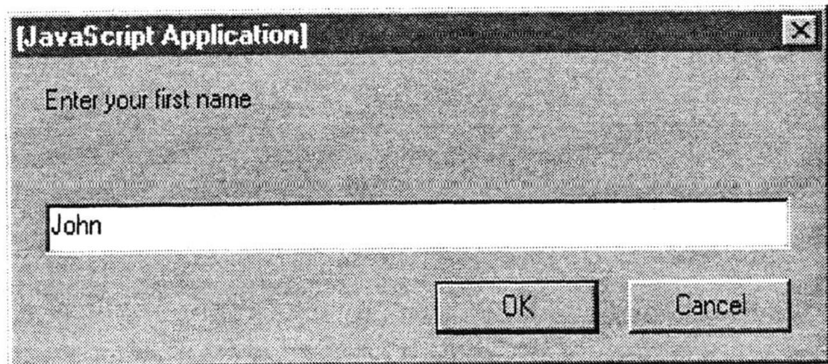


**Figure 1.5 A prompt box**

The following statement will show the box in Figure 1.5.

```
name = prompt("Enter your first name.", "")
```

If the second argument is supplied, it automatically enters into the text field at the bottom. It is also highlighted. Pressing the Del key will erase it. If you just start typing, it will go away. If you just click OK, this default entry is supplied. If this argument is an empty string as in our case, the entry field is empty. If you supply no argument in the statement, then the "undefined" string becomes the default entry.

The entry supplied by the user is assigned to a variable. If nothing is supplied and OK is clicked (or Enter pressed), then the variable holds an empty string. If Cancel is clicked instead, the `null` value is returned.

The confirm box takes one argument and returns a value. The following statement will produce Figure 1.6.

```
result = confirm("Are you sure?")
```

If you choose OK, **true** is returned. If you choose Cancel, **false** will be assigned to the variable.

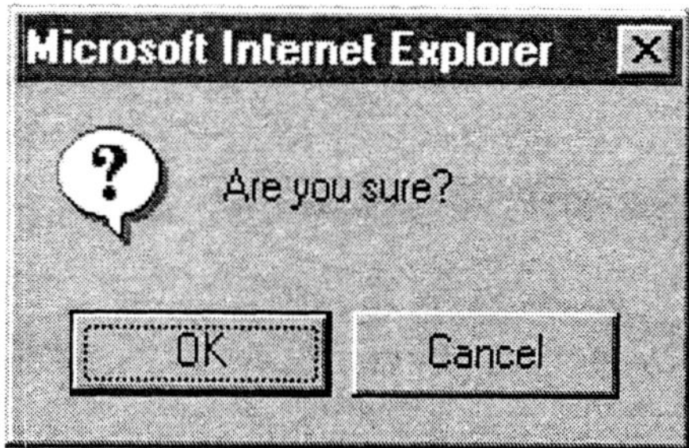


**Figure 1.6 A confirm box**

The following example will show boxes similar to those shown above:

```
<HTML>
<HEAD>
<TITLE>Dialog boxes demo</TITLE>
</HEAD>
<BODY>
<SCRIPT LANGUAGE="JavaScript">
<!--
  alert("Hello, welcome to my page.")
  name = prompt("Enter your first name.", "")
  result = confirm("So you are " + name + ".")
  if (result)  //if OK
    {alert("You are telling the truth.")}
  else  //if Cancel
    {alert("You are not telling the truth.")}
//-->
</SCRIPT>
</BODY>
</HTML>
```

# Handling Events

JavaScript, like other GUI languages, is **event-driven**. An event is something that occurs. It could be generated by the browser or the user. For example, the browser's loading and unloading a page will lead to the **onload** and **onunload** events.

Mostly, however, events are triggered by the user. When you click a push button, for example, the **onclick** event is triggered.

What happens when a button is clicked? It depends on whether there is code to respond to it. If none exists, nothing happens—the button just sits there no matter how many times or how hard you click it. If you've attached code to the button's **onclick** event, the code will be executed.

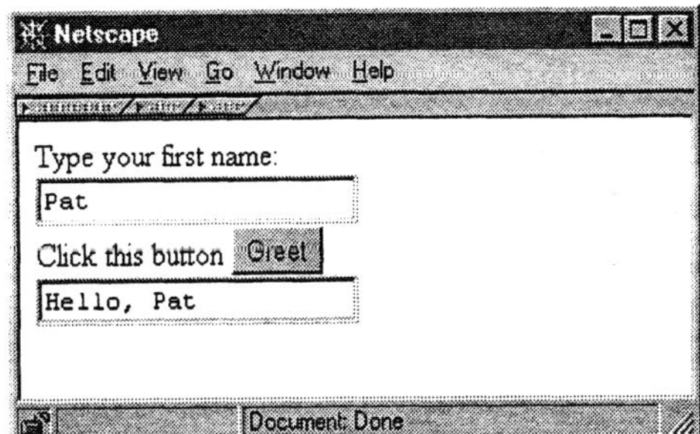


**Figure 1.7 Form objects and event handling**

An event can be handled with **inline code**. Below is an example. It produces the display shown in Figure 1.7.

```
<HTML>
<BODY>
<FORM NAME="form1">
Type your first name:<BR>
<INPUT TYPE="text" NAME="txtName"><BR>
Click this button
<INPUT TYPE="button" VALUE="Greet" onclick=
"form1.txtGreet.value='Hello, ' + form1.txtName.value">
<BR>
<INPUT TYPE="text" NAME="txtGreet">
</FORM>
</BODY>
</HTML>
```

Notice how single quotes are nested by double quotes. We can reverse the two, putting single quotes outside and double quotes inside. You can use double quotes to nest single quotes, which in turn can nest double quotes, and so on.

In this example, when the push button's **onclick** event is triggered (when you click the button), the statement after the equal sign is executed. You can place multiple statements here, with each separated from the next by a semicolon (;). These statements must also stay in one line and not broken up.

When our inline code is executed, the text entered in the first text box will be added to "Hello" and the combined string will appear in the second text box.

Inline code can be confusing. A better alternative is to place all the statements in a **function**. In the following source file, which will produce the same result as before, the event-handling code is moved to a separate function.

```
<HTML>
<HEAD>
<SCRIPT LANGUAGE="JavaScript">
<!--
  function greet()
  {
    document.form1.txtGreet.value = "Hello, " +
    document.form1.txtName.value
  }
//-->
</SCRIPT>
</HEAD>
<BODY>
<FORM NAME="form1">
Type your first name:<BR>
<INPUT TYPE="text" NAME="txtName"><BR>
Click this button
<INPUT TYPE="button" VALUE="Greet" onclick="greet()"><BR>
<INPUT TYPE="text" NAME="txtGreet">
</FORM></BODY>
</HTML>
```

**NOTE** JavaScript is case sensitive. You can use object (or variable) names in any case you want. But you must be consistent. JavaScript will treat myobj, myObj, and MyObj as all unequal. HTML, on the other hand, will accept any case.

In this arrangement, when the button is clicked, the function named `greet()` will be called (executed).

Notice the way objects are referenced. You have to follow their hierarchical order to correctly refer to them. In our case, the form named `form1` is a child of the `document` object. The objects `txtGreet` and `txtName` are children of the form. So, in order to reference a text box's property, we have to use this string:

```
document.form1.txtGreet.value
```

# Functions

A **function** is a block of program statements that are packaged as a distinct unit with a distinct name. This function can be **called** (executed) from different places again and again. Calling this function will execute it only and not other parts of the script.

## Function Basics

A function is defined with the **function** keyword, followed by a name, and ending with a pair of parentheses, like this:

```
function funcX()
{
   statements
}
```

You must also use a pair of curly braces to mark the beginning and the end of the function body. Inside the function body, you can end each statement with a semicolon. That's optional if the statement ends with a carriage return. A carriage return also serves as a statement terminator. If you want to put two statements in one line, a semicolon is required to separate them.

A function name, like a variable name (Chapter 2), is an identifier. An **identifier** must start with an alphabetic letter, not a number. A number can be inside it. Space and arithmetic operators are not allowed. You can use the underscore (_) character or case variations to make an identifier readable or meaningful.

Below is a function example. It leads to Figure 1.8.

```
<HTML>
<HEAD>
<SCRIPT LANGUAGE="JavaScript">
<!--
  function calcIt()
  {
    var num1, num2
    num1 = Number(document.form1.txtNum1.value)
    num2 = Number(document.form1.txtNum2.value)
    document.form1.txtSum.value = num1 + num2
  }
//-->
</SCRIPT>
</HEAD>
```

```
<BODY>
<FORM NAME="form1">
Enter operand 1:
<INPUT TYPE="text" NAME="txtNum1" SIZE=8><BR>
<!--allows 8 characters in the box-->
Enter operand 2:
<INPUT TYPE="text" NAME="txtNum2" SIZE=8><BR>
<INPUT TYPE="button" VALUE="Add" onclick="calcIt()">
<INPUT TYPE="text" NAME="txtSum">
</FORM>
</BODY>
</HTML>
```

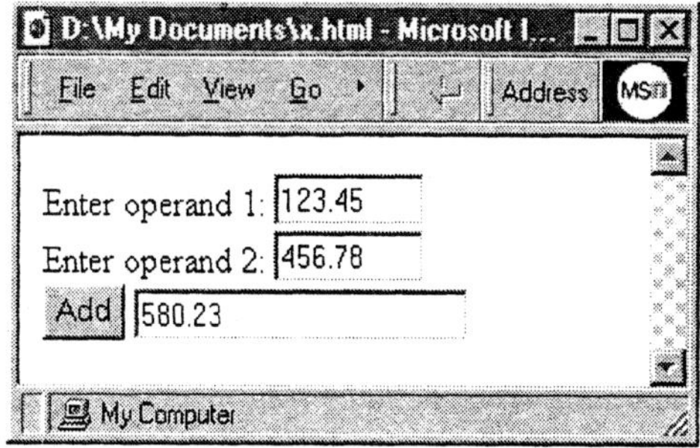


**Figure 1.8 Adding numbers**

Our function includes two variables declared with the **var** statement. A variable can also be used without declaration. A variable can hold different types of data on different occasions. See Chapter 2 for more details.

A number entered into a text box becomes the **value** property of the object. This number is treated as a text string. So we need to convert it to a numeric with the built-in **Number** (must be capitalized) function. Without this conversion, the + operator will concatenate (rather than add up) the two numbers.

## Passing Arguments

You can **pass arguments** (parameters) to a function, which in turn can do something to them.

As an example, our previous script could be modified as follows:

```
function calcIt(num1, num2)
{
  var sum
  sum = num1 + num2
  document.form1.txtSum.value = num1 + " + " +
  num2 + " = " + sum
}
. . .
<INPUT TYPE="button" VALUE="Add" onclick="calcIt(12, 34)">
```

When the button is clicked this time, the bottom text box will show this:

12 + 34 = 46

Two numbers are passed to the function. These numbers are assigned to the **num1** and **num2** variables. These are then added up and assigned to the **sum** variable. Then the string concatenation produces the text box output.

You can pass multiple arguments to a function. Just separate each argument with a comma. The giving and receiving sides must match in the number of arguments (separated with commas). Otherwise, things can go wrong.

If you want to calculate user-supplied numbers, this arrangement will work:

```
function calcIt(num1, num2)
{
  document.form1.txtSum.value = Number(num1) +
  Number(num2)
}
. . .
<INPUT TYPE="button" VALUE="Add" onclick=
"calcIt(form1.txtNum1.value, form1.txtNum2.value)">
```

In passing arguments, you can use the **this** keyword to signify the current object and **this.form** to mean the current form. Here is an example:

```
<HTML>
<HEAD>
<SCRIPT LANGUAGE="JavaScript">
<!--
  function calcIt(num)
  {
    document.form1.text2.value = num + " = " + eval(num)
  }
//-->
</SCRIPT>
</HEAD>
<BODY>
```

```
<FORM NAME="form1">
Enter a math expression and click the window:<BR>
<INPUT TYPE="text" NAME="text1""
onchange="calcIt(this.value)"><BR>
<INPUT TYPE="text" NAME="text2">
</FORM>
</BODY>
</HTML>
```

The **this** keyword represents the current control. So **this.value** is the current value entered into the text box. This value is now passed to **num**. So there is no need to assign a value to this variable.

The **onchange** event occurs to a text box when the content is changed and the **focus** goes to another object. The **onblur** event will also work in our situation. The latter event occurs whenever the involved object loses the focus.

The **eval** function is an independent built-in function (not associated with any object). It can evaluate an arithmetic expression to produce an output.

You can pass an entire object and let the function manipulate it. In that case, just use the **this** keyword, like the following:

```
<HTML>
<HEAD>
<SCRIPT LANGUAGE="JavaScript">
<!--
  function calcIt(objX)
  {
    var num = objX.value
    document.form1.text1.value = num + " = " + eval(num)
  }
//-->
</SCRIPT>
</HEAD>
<BODY>
<FORM NAME="form1">
Enter a math expression and click the window:<BR>
<INPUT TYPE="text" NAME="text1""
onchange="calcIt(this)">
</FORM>
</BODY>
</HTML>
```

In our situation, **objX** is the same as **form1.text1**. So **objX.value** holds the same value as **form1.text1.value**.

You can use **this.form** to pass the current form to a function. The function then can access anything related to that form, like this:

```
<HTML>
<HEAD>
<SCRIPT LANGUAGE="JavaScript">
<!--
  function calcIt(frmX)
  {
    var num = frmX.text1.value
    frmX.text1.value = num + " = " + eval(num)
  }
//-->
</SCRIPT>
</HEAD>
<BODY>
<FORM NAME="form1">
Enter a math expression and click the window:<BR>
<INPUT TYPE="text" NAME="text1""
onchange="calcIt(this.form)">
</FORM>
</BODY>
</HTML>
```

In our case, **this.form** is the same as **document.form1**. This form is passed to variable **frmX**. Notice that in the function we have replaced **document.form1** with **frmX**. Either one will work in this situation. Here we have two names pointing to the same thing.

**NOTE** The two browsers handle forms and form objects quite differently. In Internet Explorer, you can skip the <FORM> and </FORM> tags. Netscape Navigator will refuse to display form objects without these tags.

Internet Explorer allows you to attach custom properties to a form object, but Netscape Navigator won't allow that. Consider this statement:

```
<INPUT TYPE="button" myAge=30 VALUE="Show Age"
onclick="alert(this.myAge)">
```

Internet Explorer will show 30 in the alert box. So myAge is treated as a property of the object. Netscape Navigator will display the "undefined" message; so it doesn't recognize this additional property. In Internet Explorer, you can also use myAge alone (without "this") or pass either (with or without "this") to a function. You can even embed multiple custom properties in an object.

## Returning Values

After a function finishes processing, you can make it return a value. The function and the calling statement must be kept in sync, as shown below:

```
<HTML>
<BODY>
<SCRIPT LANGUAGE="JavaScript">
<!--
  function addUp(num1, num2)
  {
    sum = num1 + num2
    return sum  //return processed result to caller
  }

  result = addUp(17, 39)
    //call function, pass arguments, demand a return
  document.write(result)  //output result
//-->
</SCRIPT>
</BODY>
</HTML>
```

This example will output 56 to the window. The caller (**addUp()**) passes two arguments and requests a return. The function itself receives two arguments, processes them, and uses the **return** statement to send back the processed result.

Our calling statement involves assigning a function name to a variable. If you just want to call a function, the variable is not needed, such as this modified version:

```
<!--
  function addUp(num1, num2)
  {
    sum = num1 + num2
    document.write(sum)  //output result
  }

  addUp(17, 39)
    //call function, pass arguments, no return
//-->
```

This will produce the same result as before. The processed result is now output to the window from inside the function. The caller no longer receives a value.

# Loading Sequence and Script Placing

A Web page can contain multiple script blocks, each enclosed in appropriate HTML tags. Unless otherwise necessary, you should group all the code in one block and put it in the head section of the page. On some occasions, however, you may need to place some code segment somewhere else.

Scripts are loaded to memory when they are encountered during page loading. A function is just loaded and not executed right away. On the other hand, statements that are not functions, such as calling a function, are executed as they are encountered. Calling a function before the function is loaded will lead to an error because the function does not yet exist. So it's a good idea to load functions first by placing them in the page's head section.

The following source file illustrate page loading sequence:

```
<HTML>
<HEAD>
<SCRIPT LANGUAGE="JavaScript">
<!--
  function alertfunc(msg)
  {
    alert(msg)
  }
  alert("loading")
//-->
</SCRIPT>
</HEAD>
<BODY onload="alert('loading complete')"
onunload="alert('leaving')">
<FORM>
Loading sequence demo.<BR>
<SCRIPT LANGUAGE="JavaScript">
<!--
    alert("body part")
      //executing a method
    alertfunc("direct function call")
      //calling a function
//-->
</SCRIPT>
<INPUT TYPE="button" VALUE="Loading Demo"
onclick="alertfunc('Clicking a button')">
<INPUT TYPE="button" VALUE="Loading Demo">
</SCRIPT>
</FORM>
</BODY>
</HTML>
```

These are the steps taken by a browser:

1. Loads the page, including the script function.
2. Executes script statements (those not enclosed in braces) as they are encountered.
3. Displays the page.
4. Triggers the **`onload`** event.

When you refresh the page (F5 in Internet Explorer and Ctrl+R in Netscape Navigator), you'll first trigger the **`onunload`** event. So our alert box will show the message. Then the above loading sequence is repeated.

We have two script statements in the body section. Since they are not enclosed in braces, they'll be executed as they are encountered in the process of loading. They also demonstrate how you can call a function without triggering an event.

# Importing Scripts

You can put a series of script statements in a separate file and import it to a Web page. The statements can then be applied to the page. This is an efficient way to manage large and complex scripts. In designing these scripts, you might want to make them portable and reuse them on multiple occasions.

Let's use the example shown two sections before. We need to take the statement in the function out of the function block and save it to a separate file. This is the statement:

```
document.form1.text1.value = num + " = " + eval(num)
```

Cut and paste it to another instance of Notepad and save it as **`myscript.js`**. Here the extension is optional (you can also use another extension) but useful as a reminder.

A script file must contain only statements that the browser's language engine can understand and execute. Anything else, such as HTML tags and regular text, will lead to errors.

In the page where you want to bring in a script file, use the SRC attribute with the <SCRIPT> tag, such as this example:

```
<HTML>
<HEAD>
<SCRIPT SRC="myscript.js">
</SCRIPT>  //importing an external script file
</HEAD>
<BODY>
<FORM NAME="form1">
Enter a math expression and click the window:<BR>
<INPUT TYPE="text" NAME="text1""
onchange="calcIt(this.value)">
</FORM>
</BODY>
</HTML>
```

The bottom part of the page is the same as before. Here we try to call a function that is imported in the <HEAD> block.

The </SCRIPT> tag is necessary to mark the end of the element. Also, anything placed between <SCRIPT> and </SCRIPT> will be ignored. If you want to import another file, use another block like this with a different file name. If you want to add a local script, use another block like this without the SRC attribute.

# Drill

____ 1. This tag will display text in a monospaced font:
- a. <H1>
- b. <P>
- c. <PRE>
- d. <FONT>

____ 2. The text displayed by <H6> is larger than that displayed by <H1>. True or false?

____ 3. An HTML comment is added with this:
- a. //. . .
- b. /*. . .*/
- c. <!--. . .-->
- d. any of the above
- e. none of the above

____ 4. In the following statement, the resulting alert box will show:

```
<INPUT TYPE="button" VALUE="Click Here"
onclick="alert(this.type)">
```

a. "Click Here"
b. "button"
c. "INPUT"
d. an error
e. nothing

____ 5. A(n) _________ contains methods, properties, and events.

____ 6. Fill in the missing attribute in the following statement:

```
<SCRIPT _____="script1.js"></SCRIPT>
```

____ 7. The onload event handler is placed within this tag:
a. <BODY>
b. <FORM>
c. <HEAD>
d. any of the above

____ 8. The onunload event is triggered when the current page is refreshed. True or false?

____ 9. The ______ function evaluates an arithmetic expression and returns a numeric result.

____ 10. Suppose you have the following scenario, and 1 and 2 are entered into the two text boxes. The sum variable will have the value of 3. True or false?

```
x = document.form1.text1.value
y = document.form1.text2.value
sum = x + y
```

ANSWERS: 1.c; 2.F; 3.c; 4.b; 5.object; 6.SRC; 7.a; 8.T; 9.eval; 10.F

# Practice

◙ 1. What does the following statement do?

```
<INPUT TYPE="button" VALUE="Click Here"
onclick="alert('You clicked me.')">
```

2. Explain what the following script will do.

```
<SCRIPT>
<!--
 document.write ("<H1>Hello, world!</H1>")
-->
</SCRIPT>
```

3. Explain what the following source file will do.

```
<HTML>
<HEAD>
<SCRIPT LANGUAGE="JavaScript">
<!--
 document.write ("<H1>Hello, world!</H1>")
//-->
</SCRIPT>
</HEAD>
<BODY>
<H1>Hello, world!</H1>
<SCRIPT LANGUAGE="JavaScript">
<!--
 document.write ("<H1>Hello, world!</H1>")
//-->
</SCRIPT>
</BODY>
</HTML>
```

4. Create a push button with the "Hello" caption. When the button is clicked, it should show two consecutive alert boxes, with the first showing "Hello 1" and the second showing "Hello 2." The event should be handled with inline code.

5. Do the same thing as in the previous question, except that the event handler should call two separate functions and pass the two separate messages to the functions.

6. Do the same thing as in the previous question, except that the two functions should be reduced to one, the two calling statements should pass "1" and "2"

to the function, and the function should then produce "Hello 1" and "Hello 2" in the alert boxes.

7. Explain the argument passing mechanism in the following source file.

```
<HTML>
<HEAD>
<SCRIPT LANGUAGE="JavaScript">
<!--
 function greet(myForm)
 {
   myForm.txtGreet.value = "Hello, " +
   myForm.txtName.value
 }
//-->
</SCRIPT>
</HEAD>

<BODY>
<FORM NAME="form1">
Type your first name:<BR>
<INPUT TYPE="text" NAME="txtName"> <BR>
<INPUT TYPE="button" VALUE="Greet"
onclick="greet(this.form)"> <BR>
<INPUT TYPE="text" NAME="txtGreet">
</FORM>
</BODY>
</HTML>
```

8. Explain how `this` and `this.form` differ.

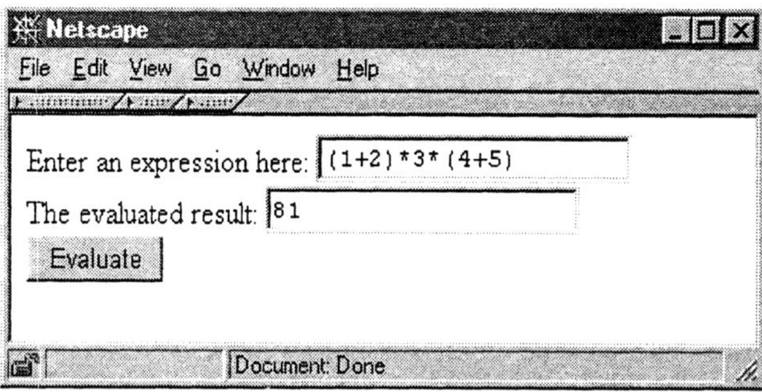


**Figure 1.9 Evaluating an expression**

■ 9. Create an interface shown in Figure 1.9. When the Evaluate button is clicked, the arithmetic expression entered into the first text box should be evaluated and the result should be shown in the second text box. When the onclick event handler calls a function, no argument should be passed.

■ 10. Do the same thing as in the previous question, except that the current form should be passed to the function, which in turn should manipulate the passed form and its objects.

# Answers

1. It will create a push button with the "Click Here" caption. When the button is clicked, an alert box will appear to show the "You clicked me" message.

2. In Internet Explorer, it'll work just fine--it will output a text string to the window. In Netscape Navigator, the --> line will be considered an error because it's not a valid JavaScript statement. You need to precede it with the // (comment) sign to hide it.

   The absence of LANGUAGE="JavaScript" won't cause any problem with either browser because "JavaScript" is the default script language for both browsers.

3. "Hello, world!" will be printed to the window three times, the first time by a script statement in the <HEAD> block, the second time by an HTML tag at the beginning of the <BODY> block, and the third time by another script statement at the end of the <BODY> block.

4. <INPUT TYPE="button" VALUE="Hello" onclick="alert('Hello 1'); alert('Hello 2')">

5.

```
<HTML>
<HEAD>
<SCRIPT LANGUAGE="JavaScript">
<!--
 function alertbox1(msg)
 {alert(msg)}

 function alertbox2(msg)
 {alert(msg)}
//-->
</SCRIPT>
```

```
</HEAD>
<BODY>
<FORM>
<INPUT TYPE="button" VALUE="Hello"
onclick="alertbox1('Hello 1'); alertbox2('Hello 2')">
</FORM>
</BODY>
</HTML>
```

6.

```
<HTML>
<HEAD>
<SCRIPT LANGUAGE="JavaScript">
<!--
 function alertbox(msg)
 {alert("Hello " + msg)}
//-->
</SCRIPT>
</HEAD>
<BODY>
<FORM>
<INPUT TYPE="button" VALUE="Hello"
onclick="alertbox('1'); alertbox('2')">
</FORM>
</BODY>
</HTML>
```

7. We use the "this.form" notation to pass a value to a function. This particular notation means the current form. When the function is executed, myForm holds the value of the current form. In this case, we no longer need to use "document" to reference this particular form.

8 `this` represents the current object. So if a push button is clicked, "this" represents the clicked button. If this object is passed to a function, the function has access to the object's properties. If the object is not passed to the function, then the function has to reference the object by the entire hierarchy, such as document.form1.button1.value.

   `this.form` refers to the current form. Suppose you click a button and pass this expression to a function, the function will have access to the entire form. Suppose the form is passed from "this.form" to aForm in the function. The function can reference a text box in the form with something like aForm.text1.value. Without passing the form, the function will have to reference the same form with the whole hierarchical string, such as document.form1.text1.value.

9.

```
<HTML>
<HEAD>
<SCRIPT LANGUAGE="JavaScript">
<!--
 function evaluate()
 {
   var num = document.form1.txtInput.value
   document.form1.txtOutput.value = eval (num)
 }
//-->
</SCRIPT>
</HEAD>
<BODY>
<FORM NAME="form1">
Enter an expression here:
<INPUT TYPE="text" NAME="txtInput"> <BR>
The evaluated result:
<INPUT TYPE="text" NAME="txtOutput"> <BR>
<INPUT TYPE="button" VALUE="Evaluate"
onclick="evaluate()">
</FORM>
</BODY>
</HTML>
```

10.

```
<HTML>
<HEAD>
<SCRIPT LANGUAGE="JavaScript">
<!--
 function evaluate(form)
 {
   var num = form.txtInput.value
   form.txtOutput.value = eval(num)
 }
//-->
</SCRIPT>
</HEAD>
<BODY>
<FORM>
```

```
Enter an expression here:
<INPUT TYPE="text" NAME="txtInput"> <BR>
The evaluated result:
<INPUT TYPE="text" NAME="txtOutput"> <BR>
<INPUT TYPE="button" VALUE="Evaluate"
onclick="evaluate(this.form)">
</FORM>
</BODY>
</HTML>
```

JavaScript * QuickStart

# <2> Programming Basics

This chapter covers the basic concepts and techniques of computer programming as implemented in JavaScript. If you are a complete novice, you should pay a great deal of attention here. If you are an experienced programmer, much of what is said here will sound familiar to you. If you already know C or C++, you can skip most of this chapter.

A computer language mimics a human language. In a human language, a noun or pronoun is combined with another to form an expression. So "you and me" becomes a phrase. In a computer language, variables and values are combined to become an **expression**. So a + b is an expression, the equivalent of a phrase. Here the values of variable a and variable b are added up by connecting them with an operator. On the other hand, c = a + b becomes a **statement**, which is a complete instruction like a sentence. Here we want the combined value to store in variable c.

A computer program consists of a series of statements. Each statement involves some sort of action words to manipulate expressions. These built-in keywords have special meanings like verbs in the English language. The following bsections explore these keywords.

## Variables and Scope

An **identifier** is a name you use to identify something. This something can be functions (see Chapter 1) or objects such as a form or a control. A **variable** is an identifier you use to temporarily store data in the computer's memory.

A variable name has to start with a letter, not a number or some other characters. Numbers can be embedded in a name, such as **`var1`** or **`var2xyz`**. But **`2var`** is not legal. Avoid most non-letter characters found on your keyboard. Most have special meanings that could lead to some actions of their own. So a+b or a/b should definitely be avoided.

You can use any case combination in a variable name. But different cases are distinguished and thus not interchangeable. So **varName** is different from **Varname**. You can use either one, but you must be consistent.

Some words are **reserved**. They have special meanings to the browser. You cannot use them as variable names. So **var** or **for** cannot be used alone as variable names. However, they can be embedded in variable names. So **varX** or **forSale** is legal.

JavaScript is a **loosely typed** language. A variable can be used to store different types of data on different occasions. A **strongly typed** language won't allow these kinds of use.

Variables can be used without declaration. If you wish, you can declare it first. Declaring a variable first may be a good idea because it forces a strict discipline on you. So the following three are all legal:

```
var1 = 123      //no declaration
var var1 = 123        //declare and use
var var1        //declare first
var1 = 123      //assign a value
```

A number enclosed in quotes becomes a text string, not a numeric. In the following scenario, the second variable holds a text string:

```
var x = 123, y = "123"
```

Using the + operator to combine the above two variables will return a text string, not a numeric. So the following alert box will show 123123, not 246:

```
alert(x + y)
```

On the other hand, when other operators are used, a browser will convert a number in quotes to a numeric. Consider the following results:

```
alert(x - y)          //0
alert(x * y)          //15129
alert(x / y)          //1
```

A variable, being a memory area for storing data, has an issue of **scope**. It has to do with where it can be seen and accessed. When you use or declare a variable inside a function, the variable is said to be **local** in scope.

A local variable is available when execution reaches its scope, namely the function containing the variable. Once execution leaves the function, the variable is dead and its stored data is erased.

If you want to keep the variable alive and its stored data persistent, you can use a **global** variable, which is also known as a **script-level** variable. A global variable, once created, can be seen from any part of the same page and accessed by other functions and statements.

How do you create a global variable? Put it outside of a function. Here is an example:

```
<HTML>
<HEAD>
<SCRIPT LANGUAGE="JavaScript">
<!--
  var var_global = "global variable"

  function func1()
  {
    var var_local = "local variable"
  }
  alert(var_global)
  alert(var_local)
//-->
</SCRIPT>
</HEAD>
</HTML>
```

If you run this script, you'll first get an alert box with the "global variable" message. Then you'll get an error telling you that the var_local is not defined. The variable is clearly in the script. But since it's inside another function which is not being executed, the browser can't see it.

**NOTE** Alert boxes are useful in **debugging** (catching program errors). You can place them in various parts of a script, including functions, to see whether execution ever reaches them. You can use them to display variable values, as shown in our preceding example; it's important that you know what a variable is doing at a particular point. When you finish debugging, make sure to take out all the extraneous alert boxes.

# Operators and Precedence

**Operators** are symbols connecting variables and values to form an expression. The expression, in turn, returns a value that can be further manipulated.

## Arithmetic Operators

| Operator | Precedence | Purpose |
|---|---|---|
| ( ) | 1 | Grouping |
| - | 2 | Negation |
| * / | 3 | Multiplication, division |
| % | 3 | Modulo arithmetic |
| + - | 4 | Addition, subtraction |

Normally, when multiple operands and operators are grouped together in an arithmetic expression, evaluation proceeds from left to right. But if an operator has a higher order of precedence, then it's evaluated first. Here are some examples and their results:

```
x = 1 + 2 * 3          // x = 7
x = (1 + 2) * 3        // x = 9
x = 11 % 2 * 3         // x = 3
x = 11 % (2 * 3)       // x = 5
```

**Modulo** arithmetic returns the remainder of the first operand divided by the second operand. So 10 % 2 returns 0, and 11 % 2 returns 1.

## Assignment Operators

The programming languages derived from C have many unconventional operators used for assigning and incrementing/decrementing values. They differ greatly from what you are familiar with in arithmetics or algebra.

When you want to assign a value to a variable, use the = sign, such as this:

```
x = 10
```

This will assign 10 to the variable. That's the easiest part. But then there are other variations. In the following expressions, the left ones are the same as those shown in the comments. They produce the same results. You are free to use either.

```
x = 10
x++              //x = x + 1
++x              //x = x + 1
x--              //x = x -1
--x              //x = x -1
x += 10          //x = x + 10
x -= 10          //x = x - 10
x *= 10          //x = x * 10
x /= 10          //x = x / 10
x %= 10          //x = x % 10
```

The two expressions x++ and ++x may produce different results under some circumstances. The first adds 1 after an operation, and the second does that before an operation. Consider the following situations:

```
x = 10
y = x++          //y is 10, x is 11
x = 10
y = ++x          //y is 11, x is 11
```

If the first example, x has the value of 10 during the assignment operation. It increments by 1 after that. So, after the assignment, x holds 11 and y holds 10.

In the second example, x increments by 1 before the operation. After the assignment, both variables have the value of 11.

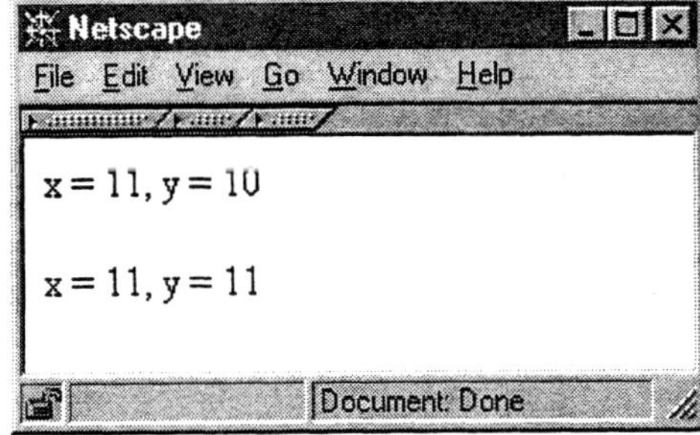


**Figure 2.1 Incrementing variables' values**

The following code, which produces Figure 2.1, proves the point:

```
<HTML>
<BODY>
<SCRIPT LANGUAGE="JavaScript">
<!--
  var x, y
  x = 10
  y = x++
  document.write ("x = ", x, ",  y = ", y)
  document.write ("<P>")
  x = 10
  y = ++x
  document.write ("x = ", x, ",  y = ", y)
  //-->
</SCRIPT>
</BODY>
</HTML>
```

You can use a single statement to assign a value to multiple variables, like this:

```
x = y = 10
```

After the assignment, both variables will have the same value, namely 10.

## Comparison and Logical Operators

Comparison operators are used to compare two values. Program execution then depends on the outcome of the comparison. Here are the comparison operators:

| | |
|---|---|
| == | Equal |
| != | Not equal |
| > | Greater than |
| >= | Greater than or equal to |
| < | Less than |
| <= | Less than or equal to |
| ? | Ternary operator, shorthand for `if` |

**NOTE** Use == for comparison and a single = for assignment. Don't get them confused.

A comparison operator is placed between two values to determine whether the result is `true` or `false`. These two words are built into JavaScript. These are known as **Boolean** values. You can assign either value to a variable, which then becomes a Boolean variable.

In the following example, the first alert box will show "false" and the second will produce "true".

```
<HTML>
<BODY>
<SCRIPT LANGUAGE="JavaScript">
<!--
  var x = 10, y = 11
  alert("'x == y' = " + (x == y))   //false
  alert("'x != y' = " + (x != y))   //true
//-->
</SCRIPT>
</BODY>
</HTML>
```

The **&&** (logical And) and || (logical Or) operators are often used to compare two expressions and return **true** or **false**. In the following scenario, our alert box will show B. If the score is outside of the specified range, 80 for example, no alert box will appear.

```
<HTML>        <!--Listing 1-->
<BODY>
<SCRIPT LANGUAGE="JavaScript">
<!--
  var score = 77
  if ((score >= 70) && (score < 80))
    {alert("B")}
//-->
</SCRIPT>
</BODY>
</HTML>
```

The above example requires both conditions (expressions) to be true. If you want only one condition to be true, use the || operator. In the following scenario, you'll qualify if you are either married or 21 or older:

```
<HTML>        <!--Listing 2-->
<BODY>
<SCRIPT LANGUAGE="JavaScript">
<!--
  var age = 20
  var mstatus = "single"
  if ((age >= 21) || (mstatus == "married"))
    alert("You qualify.")
  else
    alert("You don't qualify.")
//-->
</SCRIPT>
</BODY>
```

```
</HTML>
```

Since you are 20 and single, you don't meet either condition. So the second alert box will appear.

Instead of using **if** to test a condition, you can use the **?** operator as a shorthand. Here is an example:

```
<HTML>
<BODY>
<SCRIPT LANGUAGE="JavaScript">
<!--
  var result, a = 10, b = 9
  result = (a > b) ? "A greater than B" : "B greater than A"
  alert (result)
//-->
</SCRIPT>
</BODY>
</HTML>
```

In our situation, the condition (a > b) is true, so the first value, the one before the colon, is assigned to the variable.

We could use an **if-else** construct to replace this situation. That will be demonstrated in the next section.

# Branching with `if`

The **if** statement is used for **branching**, allowing you to choose one branch or the other to execute. The **else** branch is optional, depending on what you want to test.

This is the basic prototype:

```
if (condition)
   {statement}
else
   {statement}
```

In an **if** statement, a condition is placed inside a pair of parentheses. If the condition is true (returning the **true** value), the ensuing statement is executed. If there is a single statement, braces are optional. If there are multiple lines, you must enclose them in a pair of braces. If the condition is not true (returning the **false** value), the **else** branch is executed. Again, if there are multiple lines, enclose them in braces.

The following source file will produce a display with a text box and a push button. You are asked to enter a grade point into the text box and click the button. If the number you supply is 3 or higher, the "You qualify" message will appear. Otherwise, the "You don't qualify" message will show up.

```
<HTML>
<HEAD>
<SCRIPT LANGUAGE="JavaScript">
<!--
  function calcIt(num)
  {
    if (num >= 3)
      {alert("You qualify")}
    else
      {alert("You don't qualify")}
  }
//-->
</SCRIPT>
</HEAD>
<BODY>
<FORM>
Enter your GPA here:<BR>
<INPUT TYPE="text" NAME="txtGPA"><BR>
Click this button:<BR>
<INPUT TYPE="button" VALUE="Calculate"
onclick="calcIt(txtGPA.value)">
</FORM>
</BODY>
</HTML>
```

You can embed in the **`if`** or **`else`** branch another **`if-else`** construct to test more conditions.

# Branching with `switch`

If you have multiple choices rather than one or two, use the **`switch`** statement to do branching. You use it to match a test expression to one of the available labels. If a label matches, then the ensuing block of statements is executed while the others are ignored.

A switch construct follows this prototype:

```
switch (expression)
{
  case label1:
```

```
      statement1
      statement2
      break
    case label2:
      . . .
    default:
      statement1
      statement2
  }
```

The test expression can be a variable or an expression that returns a value. It is enclosed in parentheses, like the one in an **if** construct. Then a series of "case *label*:" lines mark different blocks of statements. If the expression matches a particular label, the statements in that block are executed. The others are ignored.

Here is an example:

```
<HTML>
<HEAD>
<SCRIPT LANGUAGE="JavaScript">
<!--
  function calcIt(num)
  {
    if (num > 4 || num < 1)
      {
        alert("Out of range")
        return  //get out of function
      }

    switch (num)
    {
    case "1":
      alert("Choice: " + "1")
      break
    case "2":
      alert("Choice: " + "2")
      break
    case "3":
      alert("Choice: " + "3")
      break
    case "4":
      alert("Choice: " + "4")
      break
    }
  }
//-->
</SCRIPT>
</HEAD>
<BODY>
<FORM>
```

```
Enter 1 - 4 here:<BR>
<INPUT TYPE="text" NAME="txtChoice"><BR>
Click this button:<BR>
<INPUT TYPE="button" VALUE="Calculate"
onclick="calcIt(txtChoice.value)">
</FORM>
</BODY>
</HTML>
```

Our **if** block is to filter out an invalid number. If a number other than 1 - 4 is supplied, the function is exited and the code below is not executed. In the past, we have used the **return** statement to make a function return a value. Here we use it alone to break out of the function.

Our **switch** statement is followed by a variable enclosed in a pair of parentheses. This is the test expression which we want to match an available label below.

Notice that we use "1" instead of 1 in a **case** label. If you use the latter, it'll work in Netscape Navigator, but not in Internet Explorer. Internet Explorer requires a **case** label and the **switch** expression to match in data type.

The **break** statement is necessary to prevent spill over. Its absence will result in the ensuing lines being executed. Here we want to break out of this structure after some statements are executed.

If our test expression doesn't match any of the available labels, then the whole switch structure is ignored. The statements following that, if any, will then be executed.

You can specify a **default** option to tell the browser what to do if no matching label is found. So our function could be modified as follows:

```
function calcIt(num)
{
  switch (num)
  {
  case "1":
    alert("Choice: " + "1")
    break
  case "2":
    alert("Choice: " + "2")
    break
  case "3":
    alert("Choice: " + "3")
    break
  case "4":
    alert("Choice: " + "4")
    break
```

```
    default:
        alert("Out of range")
    }
}
```

We've gotten rid of the **if** structure at the beginning and added the **default** option at the end of the **switch** structure. If the user entry doesn't match any label in this list, then the **default** option is executed. Here we didn't add a **break** statement. It's unnecessary because this is the end of the **switch** structure and there is nothing left for spill over.

You can stack several labels like this:

```
case "1":
case "2":
  alert("Choice: " + "1 or 2")
  break
```

In this case, if the test expression matches either label, the block below them will be executed.

# Looping with `for`

The for statement is used for **looping**. It lets you repeatedly execute a block of statements a specified number of times. It follows this syntax:

```
for (initialize-var; condition; update-var)
   {statements}
```

There are three parts enclosed in a pair of parentheses and separated from one another with semicolons (;). The first is a statement assigning an initial value to a variable (known as a **control variable**). The second is a conditional expression (not a statement) that returns **true** or **false**. And the third is a statement to update the variable's value.

Here is a concrete example:

```
for (i = 1;  i <= 10; i++)
   {statements}
```

Here we want to use variable `i` (you can declare it first, such as **var i = 1**) to have the initial value of 1. If the second expression returns true, namely `i` is less than or equal to the value of 10, the loop is entered and the statements inside are executed. Then the last part adds 1 to the value of **i**. So **i** has the value of 2 at the end of the first loop. Then the condition (the second part) is evaluated true again and the loop is repeated once more. This continues until **i** reaches 11. At that point, the condition is no longer true, so the loop is exited.

You can loop from a higher value downward, like this:

```
for (i = 10; i <= 1; i--)
```

Here we go from 10 to 1. Make sure you understand how this differs from the previous example.

The last part is commonly known as a **step value**. You can specify a step value that is higher or lower than 1. Here is how you do it:

```
for (i = 1; i <= 10; i += 2)
```

This will lead to 1, 3, 5, 7, and 9. The **i += 2** expression is a shorthand for i = i + 2. You can use either one.

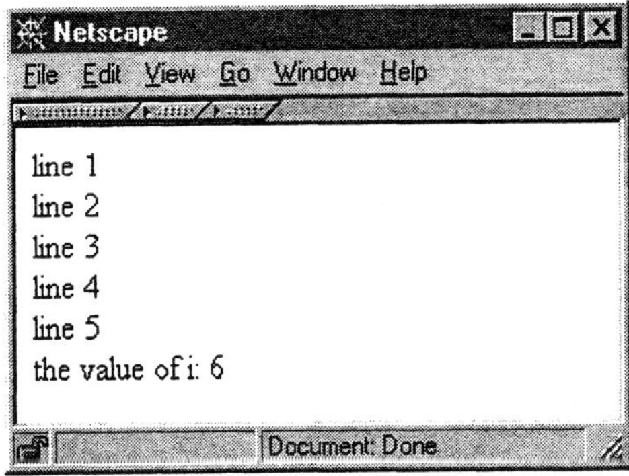


**Figure 2.2 Looping demo**

Here is a concrete example. It will output five lines to the window, as shown in Figure 2.2.

```
<HTML>
<HEAD>
<SCRIPT LANGUAGE="JavaScript">
<!--
```

```
    var i
    for (i = 1; i <= 5; i++)
      {
        document.write("line " + i)
        document.write("<BR>")
      }
    document.write("the value of i: " + i)
//-->
</SCRIPT>
</HEAD>
<BODY>
</BODY>
</HTML>
```

The following statement is used to control the looping mechanism:

```
for (i = 1; i <= 5; i++)
```

Here we assign the initial value to variable **i**. We then tell the browser to continue looping when **i** is less than or equal to 5. The variable's value is to increment by 1 after each loop. When **i** reaches the value of 6, the looping mechanism is ended. At this point, **i** has the value of 6, as shown in the figure.

We can use a string concatenation technique to reduce our two lines in the **for** block to a single line, like this:

```
document.write("line " + i + "<BR>")
```

This is a useful technique if you want to combine fixed items with variables.

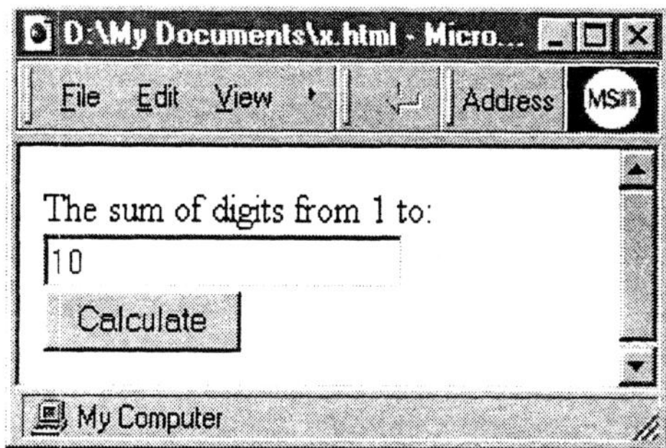


**Figure 2.3 Calculating sum of digits**

The following example produces the display shown in Figure 2.3.

```
<HTML>
<HEAD>
<SCRIPT LANGUAGE="JavaScript">
<!--
  function calcIt(num)
  {
    var i, sum = 0  //declaring two variables
    for (i = 1;  i <= num; i++)
    {
      sum = sum + i  //add each number to sum
    }
   alert("The sum of 1 to " + num + " is:" + "\n\n\t" + sum)
  }
//-->
</SCRIPT>
</HEAD>
<BODY>
<FORM>
The sum of digits from 1 to:<BR>
<INPUT NAME="txtNum"><BR>
<INPUT TYPE="button" VALUE="Calculate"
onclick="calcIt(txtNum.value)">
</FORM>
</BODY>
</HTML>
```

If 10 is passed to the function, the result is shown in Figure 2.4.

**Figure 2.4 Outputting sum of digits**

Our loop starts with 1 and continues up to the number specified in the text box. Each subsequent number is added to the **sum** variable.

We are using some **escape sequences** (\n\n\t) to format the output display. The last section in this chapter will provide details.

We can let the user specify two numbers to calculate the sum of digits from the first number to the second. Here is one way to do it:

```
<HTML>
<HEAD>
<SCRIPT LANGUAGE="JavaScript">
<!--
  var num1, num2
    //global variables
  function promptIt()
  {
    num1 = prompt("Enter the first number:", 1)
      //supply message and default value
    num2 = prompt("Enter the second number:", 10)
  }

  function calcIt()
  {
    var i, sum = 0
    for (i = num1;  i <= num2; i++)
    {
      sum = sum + parseInt(i)
    } //convert i to an integer

    alert("The sum of " + num1 + " to " + num2 + " is:" +
"\n\n\t" + sum)
  }
//-->
</SCRIPT>
</HEAD>
<BODY>
<FORM>
Click the button to calculate sum of digits:<BR>
<INPUT TYPE="button" VALUE="Calculate"
onclick="promptIt(); calcIt()">
<!--calling two functions here-->
</FORM>
</BODY>
</HTML>
```

We use two global variables to store user input numbers. These numbers then become available for the other function. If we put these variables in the first function instead, the second function cannot see these values.

We initialize the **sum** value to 0 and use the built-in **parseInt** function to convert variable **i** to an integer value. Without these extra measures, our numbers will be treated as text strings and concatenated rather than added up. If you wish to convert a value to floating point, use the **parseFloat** function instead.

The Calculate button's event handler calls two functions separated with a semicolon. This mechanism allows you to execute multiple inline statements.

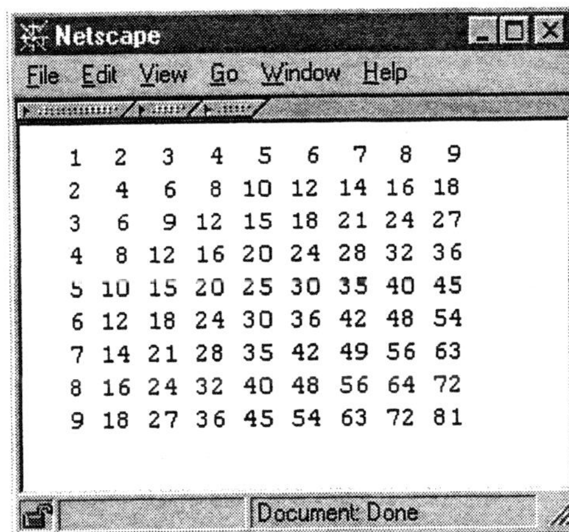


**Figure 2.5 Multiplication table**

A loop can nest another loop. As the outer loop goes through each pass, the inner loop is executed once. In the following example, the outer loop goes through nine passes, in each of which the inner loop goes through nine passes of its own. By the time the two loops are through, 81 number will be output to the window, as shown in Figure 2.5.

```
<HTML>        <!--Listing 3-->
<HEAD>
<SCRIPT LANGUAGE="JavaScript">
<!--
  document.write("<PRE>")
    //use preformatted (monospaced) font
  var i, j, total
  for (i = 1; i < 10; i++)
  {
    for (j = 1; j < 10; j++)
    {
      total = i * j
      total = " " + total
        //add 1 space to every number
```

```
        if (total < 10) total = " " + total
          //add another space before single digit
        document.write(total)
      }
      document.write("<BR>")
        //break at end of line
    }
    document.write("</PRE>")
  //-->
  </SCRIPT>
  </HEAD>
  <BODY>
  </BODY>
  </HTML>
```

You can use the **for-in** statement to loop through all the members in an object. This will be covered in Chapter 4.

# Looping with while

The **while** or **do-while** statement resembles the **for** statement in that the statements inside the block are repeatedly executed. Although a condition can be specified, there is no automatic incrementing or decrementing mechanism. These can be added by you, if you wish.

The **while** structure can take two forms:

```
while (condition)
{
  . . . .
}

do
{
  . . . .
} while (condition)
```

In the first form, the structure may be ignored completely, depending on the condition (true or false). In the second, the structure is automatically entered. So it will be executed at least once. How many more times it will be executed depends on the condition.

If the condition returns a 0 or **null** value, it will be treated as **false**. So a text string will be considered 0 and thus false.

The following example will prompt you to enter a password. A **do-while** loop gives you three chances to enter the correct password.

```
<HTML>
<HEAD>
<SCRIPT LANGUAGE="JavaScript">
<!--
  function checkPass()
  {
    var password = "opensesame"
    var num = 1
    var userpass
    do
    {
      userpass=prompt("Enter the password, try #" + num, "")
      if (userpass == password)
      {
        alert("You got it in try #" + num)
        break  //break out of loop
      }
      num++
    }
    while (num <= 3)

    if (num > 3) alert ("You failed.")
  }
//-->
</SCRIPT>
</HEAD>
<BODY>
<FORM>
Click the button to enter:<BR>
<INPUT TYPE="button" VALUE="Enter"
onclick="checkPass()">
</FORM>
</BODY>
</HTML>
```

Our loop is entered at least once. A prompt box appears. If a correct password is supplied, the **break** statement directs execution out of the loop. If not, the **while** condition is tested and the loop is repeated as long as **num** is less than 4.

The **break** statement can be used inside a **for** or **while** loop. On some occasions, you can use the **continue** statement to direct execution to the top of the loop.

We can alter our looping structure like this:

```
    while (num <= 3)
    {
```

```
    userpass=prompt("Enter the password, try #" + num, "")
    if (userpass == password)
    {
      alert("You got it in try #" + num)
      break  //break out of loop
    }
    num++
}
```

This will work the same way as before in our situation. This no longer requires the use of the **do** keyword. In this arrangement, if the initial condition is false, the whole structure will be ignored.

# Escape Sequences

All the C-family languages can handle escape sequences. An **escape sequence** is a special character preceded by a \ (backslash, also known as an **escape character**). JavaScript will respond to the following combinations:

| | |
|---|---|
| \b | backspace |
| \f | formfeed |
| \n | new line |
| \r | carriage return |
| \t | tab |
| \" | double quote |
| \' | single quote |
| \\ | backslash |

These escape sequences can be put in a text string. When the string is output to the window, a text box, or an alert box, they will format the output text.

When \ is combined with another character, such as \x, the combination has no special meaning and a browser is expected to disregard the \ character. That's the case with Netscape Navigator. But Internet Explorer will give you an error in this particular combination.

Consider the following scenario. It will lead to three lines, as shown in Figure 2.6.

```
var str = "\'line 1\'\n\t\"line 2\"\n\t\t\\line 3\\"
alert(str)
```

Figure 2.6 Escape sequence in an alert box

What happens if you write the string to the window, like this?

```
var str = "line 1\nline 2\nline 3"
document.write(str)
```

Only one line will appear. Remember that browsers are trained to ignore tabs, line breaks, and extra white spaces in the source file?

Figure 2.7 Outputting escape sequences

On the other hand, if you output with the <PRE> tag, those extraneous items will be preserved. The following script produces Figure 2.7. Notice the difference when <PRE> is involved and when it's not involved.

```
<HTML>
<BODY>
<SCRIPT LANGUAGE="JavaScript">
<!--
```

```
   var str = "He said, \n\t\"Go to \'Hale\'.\""
   document.write("<PRE>")
   document.write(str)
   document.write("</PRE>")
   document.write(str)
//-->
</SCRIPT>
</BODY>
</HTML>
```

Escape sequences can be used to format text in a single-line or multi-line text box. The latter will be covered in Chapter 3.

**NOTE** Sometimes you may get an error when you use code to output the › or ‹ character. (These signs are used in HTML tags.) One way to avoid an error in this situation is to add the \ sign before › or ‹.

# Drill

____ 1. In the following scenario, the alert box will show x to have the value of ______ .

```
x = 123
function func1()
{x = 456}
function func2()
{x = 789}
alert(x)
```

____ 2. In the following scenario, the alert box will show x to hold the value of ______ .

```
var x = 1
x++
++x
alert(x)
```

____ 3. In the following scenario, the alert box will show x to hold the value of ______ .

```
var x = 1
x++
```

```
++x
alert(x++)
```

____ 4. In the following scenario, the alert box will show y to hold the value of ______ .

```
var x = 1, y = 2
x += y
alert(y)
```

____ 5. The conditional statement below will return:

```
var result, score = 55
result = (score >= 60) ? "Pass" : "Fail"
alert (result)
```

a. Pass
b. Fail
c. an error
d. nothing

____ 6. The following loop will be entered. True or false?

```
for (i = 10; i <= 1; i++)
```

____ 7. The following loop will be entered. True or false?

```
for (i = 9; i >= 1; i--)
  {document.write(i)}
```

____ 8. In the following scenario, result will have the value of:

```
result = (10 >= 9) ? true : false
```

a. 10
b. 9
c. true
d. false
e. 0

____ 9. This is an illegal statement:
a. x + y = 10
b. x += 10

c. x *= 10
d. x = y = 10

____ 10. The following loop will be entered:

```
x = 3
while (--x)
{alert(x)}
```

a. once
b. twice
c. thrice
d. never

ANWERS: 1.123; 2.3; 3.3; 4.2; 5.b; 6.F; 7.T; 8.c; 9.a; 10.b

# Practice

1. How do local variables and global variables differ?

2. In the following scenario, what will the alert box show? Explain.

```
<HTML>
<BODY>
<FORM NAME="form1">
<SCRIPT LANGUAGE="JavaScript">
<!--
  var x = 123
//-->
</SCRIPT>
</FORM>
<FORM="form2">
<SCRIPT LANGUAGE="JavaScript">
<!--
  alert(x)
//-->
</SCRIPT>
</FORM>
</BODY>
</HTML>
```

3. In the previous script, what will happen if the two forms are reversed in order, as shown below?

```
<FORM="form2">
<SCRIPT LANGUAGE="JavaScript">
<!--
  alert(x)
//-->
</SCRIPT>
</FORM>
<FORM NAME="form1">
<SCRIPT LANGUAGE="JavaScript">
<!--
  var x = 123
//-->
</SCRIPT>
</FORM>
```

4. Explain what the following loop will do.

```
var x = 10
while (x--)
{
  document.write(x)
}
```

5. What will the following alert box show? Explain.

```
var x = 11, y = 0
while (x--)
{y += x}
alert(y)
```

6. Explain what the following loop will do.

```
for (i = 1; i <= 10; i += 2)
  {document.write(i)}
```

7. In the following scenario, explain how the user-supplied numbers will be handled.

```
var x, y
x = prompt("Enter operand 1", "")
```

```
y = prompt("Enter operand 2", "")
alert(x+y)
```

- 8. In Listing 1, use a series of if statements to return a grade A (90 or higher), B (80 to below 90), C (70 to below 80), D (60 to below 70), and F (below 60).

- 9. In Listing 2, add a Boolean variable named "parent" with the true value assigned to it. If any of the three conditions is true, then you qualify.

- 10. In Listing 3, put the statements in a function, which should be called as soon the the page is loaded.

# Answers

1. Local variables are those declared or used inside a function. They are alive and can hold values only when execution reaches that function. When the function is not executed, their values, if any, are erased. So they don't exist outside the function. Global (or script-level) variables, on the other hand, are declared or used outside of any function. They exist and can hold values after they have been executed. They can be seen throughout the same page.

2. It will show 123. Variable x is a global variable. It's visible throughout the entire page. Even though x is defined in form1, it's still visible in form2.

3. It will trigger an error. Variable x is not yet defined (not yet loaded to memory) when the alert box tries to show its value. Like a function, a variable has to be loaded to memory before it can be accessed.

4. It will write 987...210 to the window. The loop is repeated 10 times. The variable's value decrements by 1 after the loop is entered each time. The first time the loop is entered, x has the value of 10 before the entry and 9 after the entry. So 9 is printed. In the last entry, x has 1 before the entry and 0 after that, so 0 is printed. At that point, "while (0)" is the same as "while (false)". So the loop is no longer entered.

5. It will show 55. This is the same as looping from 10 to 0. So the loop is entered 11 times. If you use "--x", the loop will be entered only 10 times.

6. It will print 13579. Variable i starts with the value of 1. The test condition returns true (i less than or equal to 10). So the loop is entered and 1 is printed. Then i increments by 2 in value. The condition is tested true again. So 3 is

printed. After 9 is printed, i is incremented by 2. At that point, the condition is no longer true. So the loop is no longer entered.

7. The two numbers will be concatenated. So if you enter 12 and 34 when prompted, the alert box will show 1234. You can convert each number to a numeric like this:

```
x = Number(x)
y = Number(y)
```

After that, the alert box will show 46 instead.

8.
```
<SCRIPT LANGUAGE="JavaScript">
<!--
 var score = 77
 if (score >= 90)
   alert("A")
 if ((score >= 70) && (score < 80))
   alert("B")
 if ((score >= 60) && (score < 70))
   alert("C")
 if ((score >= 50) && (score < 60))
   alert("D")
 if (score < 60)
   alert("F")
//-->
</SCRIPT>
```

9.
```
<SCRIPT LANGUAGE="JavaScript">
<!--
 var age = 20
 var mstatus = "single"
 var parent = true
 if ((age >= 21) || (mstatus == "married") || parent)
   alert("You qualify.")
 else
   alert("You don't qualify.")
//-->
```

10.
```
<HTML>      <!--multitable.html-->
```

```
<HEAD>
<SCRIPT LANGUAGE="JavaScript">
<!--

function multitable()
{
  document.write("<PRE>")
    //use preformatted (monospaced) font
  var i, j, total
  for (i = 1; i < 10; i++)
  {
    for (j = 1; j < 10; j++)
    {
      total = i * j
      total = " " + total
        //add 1 space to every number
      if (total < 10) total = " " + total
        //add another space before single digit
      document.write(total)
    }
    document.write("<BR>")
      //break at end of line
  }
  document.write("</PRE>")
}
//-->
</SCRIPT>
</HEAD>
<BODY onload="multitable()">
</BODY>
</HTML>
```

JavaScript * QuickStart

# <3> DOM and Form

The two browsers recognize and support a series of objects related to a Web page. Web programming requires you to know and manipulate these objects. This chapter gives you an overview of these objects and then concentrates on form elements.

## Document Object Model

Netscape created a model named JavaScript Object Model to tie together all the related objects to enable its browser to handle the Web. Microsoft imitated this model, added its own innovations, and called it Internet Explorer Scripting Object Model. The two models are substantially compatible. However, there are also considerable differences. W3C (World Wide Web Consortium, the body that provides standards for the Web) has organized a working group to come up with specifications to make the two browsers more compatible. In the meantime, Web authors have to be careful and avoid using features unique to only one browser.

The **Document Object Model** (DOM), which is the term used by many people to contain all the programmatic Web objects, contains these common parts:

- Window:
    - Frame
    - History
    - Location
    - Navigator
    - Document:
        - Anchor
        - Link
        - Location
        - Form:
            - Button/Reset/Submit
            - Checkbox

File
Image
Radio
Select
Text/Textarea/Password/Hidden

Keep in mind that the above list shows only the bare minimum common between the two browsers. Each browser comes with numerous additions that are not compatible to the other browser's counterparts. Those are not covered here.

Each object in this list has properties, methods, and events. There are too many of them to list here. The common ones will surface in the following sections and the next chapter as we provide concrete examples.

These objects are organized in a hierarchical manner. Each higher-level object is a container for its lower-level objects. So Window contains all the others. Document contains one or more forms, plus other objects. A form, in turn, contains all the controls inside it.

When you want to reference a particular object, you need to use a **dot notation** by connecting the parts in the correct hierarchical order and separating each with a dot. The following refers to the content in a text box named **text1**, which is contained in a form named **form1**, which is part of the Web page:

```
window.document.form1.text1.value
```

Since **window** is the default, it can be omitted. Both the **window** and **document** objects will be covered at the beginning of Chapter 4. The remainder of this chapter concentrates on the **form** object.

# Forms and Controls

In the DOM hierarchy, a form is a child of the **document** object. The **elements** (**controls**) inside a form, in turn, are the children of the form.

A form is an area in a Web page enclosed between <FORM> and </FORM>. In this area you embed a number of HTML tags to create objects. When a browser encounters these tags, it will display visible objects. Visitors use these objects to interact with the page and the server.

There are ten controls (there are different ways to count them; some resemble each other). They can be created with the following four tags and their various attributes:

| | |
|---|---|
| **<INPUT>** | To create an input field. |
| | |
| NAME | Identifier for the control, for use by a script. |
| TYPE | Specifies different types of controls: |
| BUTTON | A push (command) button. |
| CHECKBOX | A checkbox. |
| FILE | To upload a file to the server. |
| HIDDEN | Invisible control for use by scripts. |
| IMAGE | Used with SRC to load an image; clicking this image has the same effect as clicking a Submit button; can use the ALT attribute to supply an alternate text string. |
| PASSWORD | Same as TEXT, but hides user entry. |
| RADIO | A radio (option) button. |
| RESET | A push button that clears user entries and restores defaults. |
| SUBMIT | A push button that sends user input to the server. |
| TEXT | Default type, a one-line text box. |
| VALUE | A button's caption; a one-line text box's initial content; a hidden value for a radio or checkbox button. |
| | |
| **<TEXTAREA>** | A multiline text box. |
| | |
| **<SELECT>** | A list/combo (menu) box; use the <OPTION> tag to add options inside the box. |
| | |
| **<OPTION>** | An option in a list box. |

**NOTE** Each control's attributes—plus its additional properties (for use by scripts), methods, and events—will be covered in the sections below.

The most commonly used tag is the <INPUT> tag. Not surprisingly, the controls created by these tags are often called fields, **input fields**, or form input fields. Users supply information in these fields. The information is then processed by server-side or client-side (local) scripts.

# Referencing Elements

On many occasions, we have referenced a control by using specific names, like this:

```
document.form1.text1.value
```

We can also use generic ways to reference controls by using built-in arrays. This is done by using the **`forms`** array that is a property of the **`document`** object and the **`elements`** array that is a property of the **`form`** object. These arrays, which are also objects, contain index numbers pointing to specific objects. So **`document.forms[0]`** refers to the first form (in the order of creation) and **`document.forms[0].elements[0]`** refers to the first element in the first form.

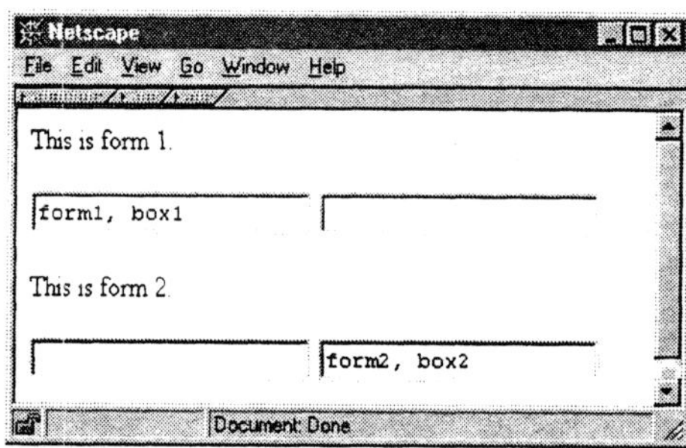


**Figure 3.1 Two forms**

Here is an example. The result is shown in Figure 3.1.

```
<HTML>
<BODY>
This is form 1.
<FORM NAME="aForm">
<INPUT TYPE="text" NAME="aText1">
<INPUT TYPE="text" NAME="aText2">
</FORM>
This is form 2.
<FORM NAME="bForm">
<INPUT TYPE="text" NAME="bText1">
<INPUT TYPE="text" NAME="bText2">
</FORM>
<SCRIPT LANGUAGE="JavaScript">
<!--
  document.forms[0].elements[0].value = "form1, box1"
  document.forms[1].elements[1].value = "form2, box2"
//-->
</SCRIPT>
</BODY>
</HTML>
```

If you want to use specific names, you'll do it this way:

```
document.aForm.aText1.value = "form1, box1"
document.bForm.bText2.value = "form2, box2"
```

This will produce the same result as the original script.

If you want to reference forms and their elements by their built-in arrays, you don't need to give them specific names.

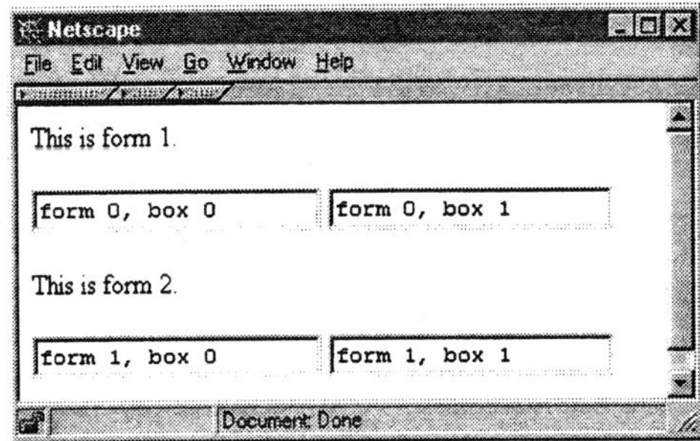


**Figure 3.2 Using a script to manage controls**

The arrays can be easily manipulated with loops, as shown below. The script will produce the display shown in Figure 3.2.

```
<HTML>
<BODY>
This is form 1.
<FORM>
<INPUT TYPE="text">
<INPUT TYPE="text">
</FORM>
This is form 2.
<FORM>
<INPUT TYPE="text">
<INPUT TYPE="text">
</FORM>

<SCRIPT LANGUAGE="JavaScript">
<!--
  var i, j
  for (i = 0; i < document.forms[0].length; i++)
  {
```

```
      for (j = 0; j < document.forms[1].length; j++)
      {
        document.forms[i].elements[j].value = "form " +
        i + ", box " + j
      }
    }
//-->
</SCRIPT>
</BODY>
</HTML>
```

We use the **length** property to end each loop. It gives us the total number of objects in an array. That's 2 in our case. Since the array is 0-based, the index ranges from 0 to 1.

We can use the **with** statement to shorten a dot notation. The following modified script will produce the same result as before:

```
<SCRIPT LANGUAGE="JavaScript">
<!--
  var i, j
  var len1 = document.forms[0].length
  var len2 = document.forms[1].length

  for (i = 0; i < len1; i++)
  {
    for (j = 0; j < len2; j++)
    {
      with(document.forms[i].elements[j])
      {
        value = "form " + i + ", box " + j
      }
    }
  }
//-->
</SCRIPT>
```

Here each **value** is a shorthand expression that is the same as this:

```
document.forms[i].elements[j].value
```

Our **with** block can be rearranged as follows. The result will not change.

```
with(document)
with(forms[i])
with(elements[j])
{
  value="form " + i + ", box " + j
}
```

In this arrangement, each child object can omit the parent object. So `forms[i]` is the equivalent of `document.forms[i]` and `elements[j]` is the same as `document.forms[i].elements[j]`.

# Events and Naming Conventions

Form controls all come with events. What events? The following list shows what W3C calls "intrinsic events." This is the exact quote from the organization's specification document (here "user agent" means a browser):

onload = script
: The onload event occurs when the user agent finishes loading a window or all frames within a FRAMESET. This attribute may be used with BODY and FRAMESET elements.

onunload = script
: The onunload event occurs when the user agent removes a document from a window or frame. This attribute may be used with BODY and FRAMESET elements.

onclick = script
: The onclick event occurs when the pointing device button is clicked over an element. This attribute may be used with most elements.

ondblclick = script
: The ondblclick event occurs when the pointing device button is double clicked over an element. This attribute may be used with most elements.

onmousedown = script
: The onmousedown event occurs when the pointing device button is pressed over an element. This attribute may be used with most elements.

onmouseup = script
: The onmouseup event occurs when the pointing device button is released over an element. This attribute may be used with most elements.

onmouseover = script
: The onmouseover event occurs when the pointing device is moved onto an element. This attribute may be used with most elements.

onmousemove = script

The onmousemove event occurs when the pointing device is moved while it is over an element. This attribute may be used with most elements.

onmouseout = script

The onmouseout event occurs when the pointing device is moved away from an element. This attribute may be used with most elements.

onfocus = script

The onfocus event occurs when an element receives focus either by the pointing device or by tabbing navigation. This attribute may be used with the following elements: LABEL, INPUT, SELECT, TEXTAREA, and BUTTON.

onblur = script

The onblur event occurs when an element loses focus either by the pointing device or by tabbing navigation. It may be used with the same elements as onfocus.

onkeypress = script

The onkeypress event occurs when a key is pressed and released over an element. This attribute may be used with most elements.

onkeydown = script

The onkeydown event occurs when a key is pressed down over an element. This attribute may be used with most elements.

onkeyup = script

The onkeyup event occurs when a key is released over an element. This attribute may be used with most elements.

onsubmit = script

The onsubmit event occurs when a form is submitted. It only applies to the FORM element.

onreset = script

The onreset event occurs when a form is reset. It only applies to the FORM element.

onselect = script

The onselect event occurs when a user selects some text in a text field. This attribute may be used with the INPUT and TEXTAREA elements.

onchange = script

The onchange event occurs when a control loses the input focus and its value has been modified since gaining focus. This attribute applies to the following elements: INPUT, SELECT, and TEXTAREA.

Notice the use of lowercase for all the event names. This is an area of considerable confusion. Netscape Navigator, following the conventions in Java, started out by using mixed case like onClick and onBlur. Most JavaScript authors follow the same convention. Microsoft mostly uses all lowercase. W3C uses all lowercase. Keep in mind that HTML is not case sensitive. So whatever case you use in HTML statements (not JavaScript statements), the case won't make any difference. In this book, we follow W3C conventions.

Names like **`onclick`** or **`onblur`** are also often called "event handlers." They are actually events. Event handlers are pieces of code that respond to events. Consider this scenario:

```
<INPUT TYPE="button" NAME="btnX" VALUE="Click Me"
onclick="calcIt()">
```

This HTML statement will create a push button with the caption of "Click Me." When this button is clicked, the function named **`calcIt()`** will be called. Here **`onclick`** is the event name and **`onclick="calcIt()"`** is the **event handler**. An event handler is a mechanism to handle an event, telling the browser what to do when the event is fired. In our case, the event is fired when the button is clicked and the event handler tells the browser to call the specified function.

The above list of events is supposed to be available to most controls. That hasn't been accomplished so far, however. The two browsers have implemented some events but not the others. Generally speaking, Internet Explorer has implemented more of the features in this list. Furthermore, the browsers have also added other events not in this list and that are ignored by the rival. When we discuss the individual controls in the following sections, we'll list only those events that have been implemented by both browsers.

# Push Buttons

**Syntax:**

<INPUT TYPE="button" | "reset" | "submit" NAME="x">

**Attributes:**

| | |
|---|---|
| VALUE | Sets the caption of the button. |
| DISABLED | Internet Explorer only. |

**Common Methods:**

blur()
click()
focus()

**Common Events**

onblur
onclick
onfocus
onmousedown
onmouseup

NOTE 1 The common methods and events are all shared by both browsers. Each browser may have additional items not shared by the other. These are not covered in this and the following sections.

NOTE 2 W3C has specified that a control can be marked with the DISABLED attribute. Such a control cannot interact with users. Internet Explorer will respond to this attribute, but Netscape Navigator won't at this time.

NOTE 3 Both browsers adjust a button's width based on the caption's width specified in the VALUE attribute. If you have a short caption, the button may become very narrow. You can add extra spaces in the caption's text string to make the button wider. In Netscape Navigator, you can use the WIDTH attribute to specify a number of pixels for the button's width. Internet Explorer won't respond to that.

There are three command buttons: **`button`**, **`reset`**, and **`submit`**. They appear alike but behave differently. They can be manipulated in similar ways. Here is an example of a **`submit`** button:

```
<INPUT VALUE="the original text" NAME="somename">
<INPUT TYPE="submit">
```

These statements will create a text box and a push button with the "Submit Query" caption (even though we didn't provide a VALUE attribute). When this button is clicked, the NAME attribute and the entry in the text box will be sent to the Web server according to the attributes specified in the <FORM> tag. If you are a server-side programmer, you need to write a programmer to capture this text. Here we concentrate on client-side programming.

The **reset** button is created this way:

```
<INPUT VALUE="the original text">
<INPUT TYPE="reset">
```

The first statement creates a text box with a default text string inside the box. The second statement creates a push button with the Reset caption. If you type something else in the text box and then click the Reset button, the original text will appear. If we didn't use the VALUE attribute to assign something, then the box will simply be empty.

You can use the VALUE attribute to specify a caption for the button: Here are two examples:

```
<INPUT TYPE="reset" VALUE="Restore the Form">
<INPUT TYPE="reset" VALUE="Clear">
```

Regardless of the caption text, the button behaves the same way as before.

The **click()** method mimics the clicking of the button. When it's executed, the function specified in the **onclick** event handler is executed. The following statement will do the same thing as your clicking the button:

```
document.form1.btnCalc.click()
```

The **onmousedown** event occurs when you click a button. The **onmouseup** (or **onclick**) event occurs when you release the button. To respond to these events, you need to use the <INPUT> tag and assign a function to either event, the same way you do with the **onclick** event. Here is an example:

```
<HTML>      <!--Listing 1-->
<HEAD>
<SCRIPT LANGUAGE="JavaScript">
<!--
  function mouseDown()
  {
    document.forms[0].elements[0].value = "Mouse Down"
  }
  function mouseUp()
  {
    document.forms[0].elements[0].value = "Mouse Up"
  }
//-->
</SCRIPT>
</HEAD>
<BODY>
<FORM>
```

```
<INPUT TYPE="button" VALUE="Click Default"
onmousedown="mouseDown()" onmouseup="mouseUp()">
</FORM>
</BODY>
</HTML>
```

Our page has only one control, a push button. It has an initial caption. When the button is clicked, another caption appears, proving that the event handler is working. When you release the button, another function will be called to display a new caption.

What happens if a button has all the three mouse-related events attached? These events occur in this order: **`onmousedown`**, **`onmouseup`**, and finally **`onclick`**.

# Text Boxes

There are four types of **text fields**: **`text`** (single line), **`textarea`** (multiline), **`password`** (typed characters appearing as asterisks), and **`hidden`** (not displayed in the browser window). They behave alike and can be used in similar ways.

## One-Line Box

**Syntax:**

<INPUT TYPE="text" | "password" | "hidden" NAME="x">

**Attributes:**

| | |
|---|---|
| MAXLENGTH | Sets the maximum number of characters allowed in the box. |
| SIZE | Sets the physical width of the box in the number of characters; 20 default. |
| VALUE | Sets the initial content in the box. |

**Additional Properties:**

| | |
|---|---|
| defaultValue | Supplies alternative content to the VALUE attribute. |

**Common Methods:**

blur()
focus()
select()

**Common Events**

onblur
onchange
onfocus
onkeydown
onkeypress
onselect

**NOTE** The W3C specification includes the READONLY attribute for a text box. Internet Explorer will respond to that in a one-line or multiline text box, Netscape Navigator won't for now. A read-only text box allows users to copy text but not alter its content, which can be changed only by a script.

A text box is created by using the <INPUT> tag alone or in combination with a series of attributes. Normally, you use this tag with a TYPE attribute. But the default type is TEXT, so there is no need to specify it.

A **password box** is created when you assign "password" to TYPE. It behaves the same way as a text box. The only difference is that when the user types something, the characters appear as asterisks. You can use SIZE to control its width and MAXLENGTH to limit the number of characters.

The NAME attribute is not needed if you just want to display a text box. But it's vital if you want to programmatically maneuver the box's content. When the form is submitted to the server, the name/value pair tells the server where the content comes from. If you want to do client-side manipulation, this name is also useful.

The default size of a text box is 20 characters in width. Netscape Navigator uses a monospaced font for such a box, so you can type exactly 20 characters in it. Internet Explorer produces a box of the same size. But since it uses a proportional font, the number of characters in this box can vary.

You can use the SIZE attribute to change the size of a text box. Keep in mind that this is not based on pixels. Instead, it's based on the number of fixed-width characters.

By default there is no limit in the number of characters you can type in a text box. If you wish you can use the MAXLENGTH attribute to specify a maximum number of input characters. Once the limit is reached, the box will refuse to accept additional characters.

The VALUE attribute specifies the initial content of the text box. This content appears when the page is loaded. The user is free to change it. After the change, the **`value`** property of the object holds the new content. This content can be programmatically manipulated. A script can also put content in a text box using the **value** property.

The **defaultValue** property (this is a script property, not an HTML attribute) can be used to store a string. This string can be an alternative to the one specified with the VALUE attribute. Consider the following scenario:

```
<HTML>
<BODY>
<FORM>
<INPUT TYPE="text" NAME="text1" VALUE="XXX">
<INPUT TYPE="reset">
<SCRIPT LANGUAGE="JavaScript">
<!--
  document.forms[0].text1.defaultValue="Box 1"
//-->
</SCRIPT>
</FORM>
</BODY>
</HTML>
```

It creates a Reset button and a text box with an initial text string (XXX). In the script, we also assign a string (Box 1) to this object's **defaultValue** property. If you now click the Reset button, the default string will replace the initial string (or the one supplied by the user). If defaultValue didn't exist in our scenario, the initial string set by VALUE will enter the box when the Reset button is clicked. So if both exist, the one set by **defaultValue** prevails.

Pressing a key when the cursor is inside a text box triggers two events: **onkeydown** first and then **onkeypress**.

The **onchange** event occurs when you change a text box's content and shift the focus to another object. On the other hand, **onblur** occurs whenever the objects loses the focus.

The **focus()** method is useful to bring the focus to a text box where users can immediately make an entry. The following script statement will bring the focus to the text box named **text1**:

```
document.form1.text1.focus()
```

You can use the **blur()** method to prevent users from changing the content in a text box. In the following example, the text box cannot receive the focus so it's not possible to change its content:

```
<INPUT TYPE="text" VALUE="You're a nut!"
onfocus="blur()">
```

**NOTE** In Internet Explorer, you can select a block of text from a text box and drag it to another text box to move the text. You can also hold down a Ctrl key as you drag. That will be copying. Netscape Navigator won't let you do that. In both browsers, you can right-click a text box to pop up a context (shortcut) menu. The available options depend on whether there is selected text. You can use these options to cut, copy, paste, undo, or undelete.

The following script demonstrates the **onblur** and **onfocus** events:

```
<HTML>       <!--Listing 2-->
<HEAD>
<SCRIPT LANGUAGE="JavaScript">
<!--
function sayHello(msg)
{
  document.myForm.txtHello.value = msg
  //or document.forms[0].elements[0].value = msg
}
//-->
</SCRIPT>
</HEAD>
<BODY>
<FORM NAME="myForm">
Click inside and outside the box:<BR>
<INPUT TYPE="text" NAME="txtHello" onfocus=
"sayHello('Hello')" onblur="sayHello('Bye')">
</FORM>
</BODY>
</HTML>
```

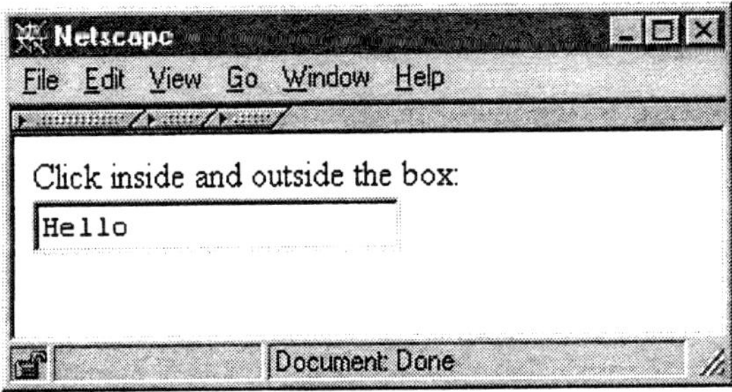


**Figure 3.3 Triggering an event**

If you now click inside the text box (Figure 3.3), the "Hello" message appears. If you click outside, the "Bye" string appears. Pressing the Tab key will also trigger these events.

## Textarea Box

**Syntax:**

<TEXTAREA>text here</TEXTAREA>

**Attributes:**

| | |
|---|---|
| COLS | Sets the number of columns in the box (default 20). |
| ROWS | Sets the number of rows in the box (default 2). |
| WRAP | "off" \| "virtual" \| "physical" |

**Additional Properties:**

| | |
|---|---|
| value | For script use only; to programmatically maneuver the content in the box. |

This control shares the same methods and events as a one-line text box (created with <INPUT TYPE="text">).

The textarea box is a multiline text-entry box. It's created with a separate <TEXTAREA> tag. Use a textarea box if you want the user to input multiline text or if you want a script to output a large amount of text.

You supply the initial text between the start and end tags, like this:

```
<TEXTAREA>initial text . . .</TEXTAREA>
```

The initial text will appear in the box created by the tag.

By default this box has two rows in height and 20 characters in width. Both browsers display text in a monospaced font. So it's easy to count how many characters can be contained horizontally.

If you don't like the default size, you can use ROWS to specify the number of rows and COLS to set the number of columns.

There is a WRAP attribute that determines how the text in the box should be displayed and submitted to the server. It has these values: OFF (no wrap; default for

Netscape Navigator), VIRTUAL (default for Internet Explorer), and PHYSICAL. These values have to do with whether or not carriage returns should be submitted to the server.

By default, the two browsers handle the textarea box very differently. If you're not aware of this, you may be in for an unpleasant surprise. The surprise comes from the different default setting for the WRAP attribute.

If you specify WRAP with no value or another value other than OFF, you can expect the two browsers to behave somewhat alike.

When WRAP is not off, a vertical scroll bar appears and a long line is automatically wrapped. So as you type a long line, the text goes down to subsequent lines without your pressing the Enter key. You can still press the Enter key to insert extra vertical spaces.

When WRAP is off, two scroll bars automatically appear. Text is not wrapped by default. If you type a long line, the horizontal scroll bar is activated. A line is wrapped only when the Enter key is pressed.

You can use the **value** property with a script to maneuver the content of a textarea box. You can thus programmatically put text there, replace it, or delete it. Keep in mind that the <TEXTAREA> tag does not include the VALUE attribute. So the **value** property can be used only in a script.

The following source code will create a textarea box and fill the box with text. The box has no initial content. The text is assigned to the **value** property of the object in a script statement.

```
<BODY>
<FORM NAME="form1">
<INPUT>
<TEXTAREA ROWS=5 COLS=30 WRAP
NAME="tarea1"></TEXTAREA>
<SCRIPT>
document.form1.tarea1.value="long text, all in one line"
</SCRIPT>
</FORM>
</BODY>
```

What happens if you click a Reset button in this situation?. The box will be cleared, restoring the default empty state. If we place some text between <TEXTAREA> and </TEXTAREA>, it will return. So the text entered this way is treated the same as the text entered into a one-line text box using the VALUE attribute.

**NOTE** Don't use the VALUE attribute with the <TEXTAREA> tag. Netscape Navigator will ignore it. Internet Explorer may get confused and refuse to execute the `value` property in a script.

A textarea object has the **`defaultValue`** property, just as a one-line text box. This property has the same relationship with the **`value`** property as discussed in the previous section.

A text string assigned to the **`value`** or **`defaultValue`** property can contain **escape sequences** such as \', \", \n, \t, and so on (see Chapter 2). Both browsers will render these. On the other hand, if these characters are in the text entered with HTML tags (i.e., not in a script), they will be displayed as they are and not rendered.

# Radio Buttons

**Syntax:**

<INPUT TYPE="radio" NAME="x">

**Attributes:**

| | |
|---|---|
| CHECKED | Sets initial checked state. |
| VALUE | Assigns a hidden value. |

**Additional Properties:**

| | |
|---|---|
| checked | Boolean true (if the button is checked) or false |
| defaultChecked | Boolean true (if marked by the SELECTED attribute) or false. |
| length | The total count of buttons sharing the same name. |

**Common Methods:**

blur()
click()
focus()

**Common Events:**

onblur
onclick
onfocus
onmousedown
onmouseup

A radio button is marked by a symbol that resembles a button on your radio. You use one <INPUT> tag to create one radio button. Multiple buttons sharing the same name let users check only one option from the group. Clicking a button selects it and enters a bullet in the circle. When the group of buttons has the focus, moving an arrow key also checks a new button and unchecks the old one.

You can have multiple groups, each with a distinct name. In each group, only one button can be checked.

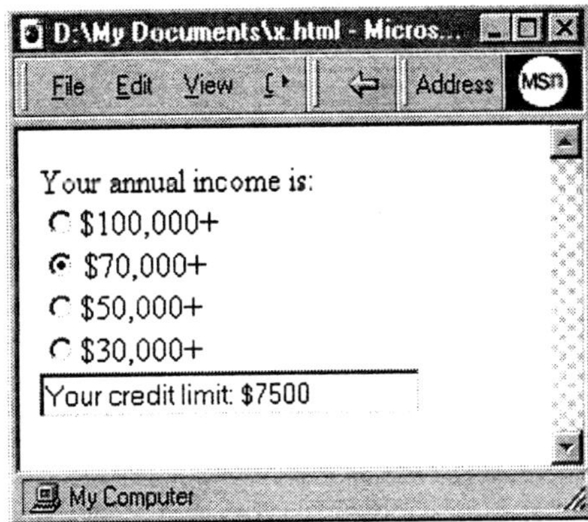


**Figure 3.4 Radio buttons**

The following example creates Figure 3.4. The third button is initially checked. Clicking another button checks it and triggers its **`onclick`** event and shows a new number in the bottom text box.

```
<HTML>
<HEAD>
<SCRIPT LANGUAGE="JavaScript">
<!--
  function showLimit(num)
  {
    var entry = document.forms[0].txtOutput
      //transfer the text box object to a variable
    entry.value = "Your credit limit: $" + num
  }
//-->
</SCRIPT>
</HEAD>
<BODY>
<FORM>
```

```
Your annual income is:<BR>
<INPUT TYPE="radio" NAME="limit" VALUE="10000"
onclick="showLimit(this.value)">$100,000+<BR>
<INPUT TYPE="radio" NAME="limit" VALUE="7500"
onclick="showLimit(this.value)">$70,000+<BR>
<INPUT TYPE="radio" NAME="limit" VALUE="5000"
CHECKED onclick="showLimit(this.value)">$50,000+<BR>
<INPUT TYPE="radio" NAME="limit" VALUE="4000"
onclick="showLimit(this.value)">$30,000+<BR>
<INPUT NAME="txtOutput" SIZE=25>
</FORM>
</BODY>
</HTML>
```

The **length** property contains the number of buttons in the group. The options in the group are stored in an array, whose name is the name of the group. In our example, we can use a loop to go through each member in the array to see which one is checked. The modified version shown below has a new push button. When it's clicked, a loop checks to see which has been selected. When one is found, the **break** statement breaks out of the loop.

```
<HTML>       <!--credit.html-->
<HEAD>
<SCRIPT LANGUAGE="JavaScript">
<!--
  function showLimit()
  {
    var group = document.forms[0].limit
      //the radio button group, an array
    var entry = document.forms[0].txtOutput
      //the text box object

    for (var i = 0; i < group.length; i++)
    {  //0-based index system
      if (group[i].checked)
        break;    //get out if checked
    }
    entry.value = "Your credit limit: $" + group[i].value
  }  //the value of the checked button
//-->
</SCRIPT>
</HEAD>
<BODY>
<FORM>
Your annual income is:<BR>
<INPUT TYPE="radio" NAME="limit" VALUE="10000">$100,000+<BR>
<INPUT TYPE="radio" NAME="limit" VALUE="7500">$70,000+<BR>
<INPUT TYPE="radio" NAME="limit" VALUE="5000">$50,000+<BR>
<INPUT TYPE="radio" NAME="limit" VALUE="4000">$30,000+<BR>
```

```
<INPUT NAME="txtOutput" SIZE=25><BR><INPUT TYPE="button"
VALUE="Check Limit" onclick="showLimit()">
</FORM>
</BODY>
</HTML>
```

The array is 0-based. So the first radio button has the index value of 0. The last one has index value of one less than the **length** property. So in our case, the length is 4 and the index goes from 0 to 3.

# Checkboxes

**Syntax:**

<INPUT TYPE="checkbox" NAME="x">

A checkbox shares the same properties, methods, and events with a radio button.

A checkbox is an input device that lets users check it to place a check mark to signify it as being selected. A group of checkboxes can share the same name. Multiple boxes can be checked, unlike a group of radio buttons. The buttons sharing the same name form an array and can thus be manipulated as in a group of radio buttons.

The following example produces Figure 3.5. Users can check multiple options. When the Calculate button is clicked. The values of the checked options will be totaled and displayed:

```
<HTML>          <!--Listing 3-->
<HEAD>          <!--order.html-->
<SCRIPT LANGUAGE="JavaScript">
<!--
  function showSum()
  {
    var group = document.forms[0].order
      //the checkbox button group, an array
    var entry = document.forms[0].txtOutput
      //the text box object
    var sum = 0

    for (var i = 0; i < group.length; i++)
    {  //0-based index system
      if (group[i].checked)
        sum += parseInt(group[i].value)
        //add up, convert value to integer
```

```
      }
      entry.value = "Order total: $" + sum
   }  //show total in text box
//-->
</SCRIPT>
</HEAD>
<BODY>
<FORM>
Check the items you wish to order:<BR>
<INPUT TYPE="checkbox" NAME="order" VALUE="10">Pizza,
$10<BR>
<INPUT TYPE="checkbox" NAME="order" VALUE="3">Sandwich,
$3<BR>
<INPUT TYPE="checkbox" NAME="order" VALUE="4">Burger, $4<BR>
<INPUT TYPE="checkbox" NAME="order" VALUE="2">Pie, $2<BR>
<INPUT NAME="txtOutput" SIZE=16>
<INPUT TYPE="button" VALUE="Calculate" onclick="showSum()">
</FORM>
</BODY>
</HTML>
```

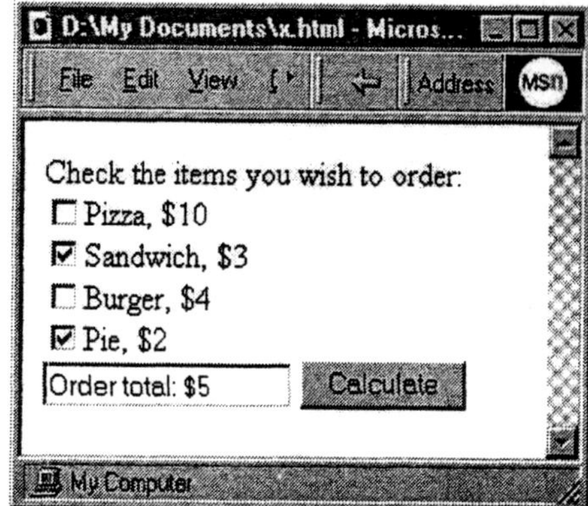


**Figure 3.5 Checkboxes**

Since a value assigned to the VALUE attribute is a text string, we need to convert it to a numeric with the **`parseInt`** function. It will lop off any decimal portion in a number. If you want to retain this portion, use **`parseFloat`** or **`Number`**.

# Select Boxes

**Syntax:**

```
<SELECT>
  <OPTION> . . .
  <OPTION> . . .
</SELECT>
```

**<SELECT> Attributes:**

| | |
|---|---|
| MULTIPLE | Allows selection of multiple options. |
| SIZE | Sets the number of options displayed (exposed) in the box. |

**<OPTION> Attributes:**

| | |
|---|---|
| VALUE | Sets a hidden value. |
| SELECTED | Sets the option as preselected (highlighted). |

**Additional Properties**

| | |
|---|---|
| length | The number of options. |
| options[ ] | An array of all the options. |
| options[ ].defaultSelected | Boolean true (if marked by the SELECTED attribute) or false. |
| options[ ].selected | Boolean true (if the option is selected) or false. |
| selectedIndex | The index value of the selected option. |
| text | Option text. |
| value | Option value. |

**Common Methods**

blur()
focus()

**Common Events**

onblur
onchange
onfocus

A select (menu, list, or combo) box supplies a list of available options. Users can select one option (maybe more). The text and value (if any) of this selection is then sent to the sever or programmatically manipulated by a local script.

By default, a select box is a combo box showing only one item. This box comes with a down arrow. Clicking this arrow (or pressing Alt and a down arrow key when the object has the focus) drops down all the available options, thus allowing the user to select one. After a selection is made, the box closes and only the selected option is shown.

The width of a select box is determined by the longest option. This cannot be changed by an attribute.

The vertical dimension can be set by the SIZE attribute of the <SELECT> tag. The number you specify determines how many options will be shown. If you specify a number less than the available number of options, the down arrow (maybe an up arrow as well) will persist. If your number is equal to or greater than the option number, the arrow will disappear and the resulting box may have some empty slots. This then becomes a list box.

By default, a select box allows only one selection among the available options. When a new one is selected by clicking or moving a cursor key and then pressing Enter, the previous option is automatically deselected.

The MULTIPLE attribute (no value) is used with the <SELECT> tag to allow the user to select multiple options. To select multiple options, hold down a Ctrl key and click each. The selected options will all be highlighted. If MULTIPLE is not used, only one option will be selected.

The SELECTED attribute (no value) is used with the <OPTION> tag to designate an option as preselected. If MULTIPLE is present, multiple options can be preselected. If not, only the last selected option will actually be selected. The preselected option (or the first) initially appears at the top of the box.

```
<HTML>
<BODY>
<FORM>
Vacation Package:<BR>
<SELECT NAME="vacation">
  <OPTION>New York
  <OPTION>Los Angeles
  <OPTION VALUE=1000>San Diego
  <OPTION>Chicago
</SELECT>
</FORM>
</BODY>
</HTML>
```

The closing </OPTION> is optional, the same as when you create a list or a table.

The above example doesn't look like much fun. You can pull down the list and click an option. But nothing happens after you select an option.

**Figure 3.6 A select box**

The following example will give you some action. As shown in Figure 3.6, you can select an option and then click the Show button to produce two entries in the bottom text boxes. You can then make another selection and click Show to produce a different result.

```
<HTML>      <!--vacation.html-->
<HEAD>
<SCRIPT LANGUAGE="JavaScript">
<!--
  function showIt(form)
  {
    var opt = form.vacation;    //list options
    var cty = opt.options[opt.selectedIndex].text
      //selected option's text
    var cst = opt.options[opt.selectedIndex].value
      //selected option's value
    form.txtCity.value = cty
      //put in text boxes
    form.txtCost.value = "$" + cst
  }
//-->
</SCRIPT>
</HEAD>
<BODY>
<FORM>
Vacation Package:<BR>
```

```
<SELECT NAME="vacation">
  <OPTION SELECTED VALUE=999>New York
  <OPTION VALUE=890>Los Angeles
  <OPTION VALUE=799>San Diego
  <OPTION VALUE=795>Chicago
</SELECT>
<INPUT TYPE="button" VALUE="Show"
onclick="showIt(this.form)">
<BR>
<INPUT TYPE="text" NAME="txtCity"><BR>
<INPUT TYPE="text" NAME="txtCost"><BR>
</FORM>
</BODY>
</HTML>
```

When the Show button is clicked, the **showIt()** function is called and the form is passed to the function. In this form the **options[]** array contains all the available options. We then use the **selectedIndex** property to tell us which option has been selected. We then try to extract the text and value of this selected option.

# Drill

____ 1. This term is used to represent the overall hierarchy of all the Web objects:
- a. DOM
- b. form
- c. control
- d. element

____ 2. A Web page can contain only one form. True or false?

____ 3. A form is a child of a:
- a. window
- b. document
- c. control
- d. none of the above

____ 4. Entering the <INPUT> tag alone and without any attribute in a Web page's source file will do nothing. True or false?

____ 5. This object is not created with the <INPUT> tag.
- a. push button
- b. radio button
- c. checkbox

d. list box

____ 6. You use the ____________ attribute to limit the number of characters allowed in a one-line text box.

____ 7. A textarea box's initial value is set by the VALUE attribute. True or false?

____ 8. A group of radio buttons sharing the same name allows only one selection. True or false?

____ 9. A group of checkboxes sharing the same name allows only one selection. True or false?

____ 10. You use the ______________ property to determine which option in a select box has been selected.

ANSWERS: 1.a; 2.F; 3.b; 4.F; 5.d; 6.MAXLENGTH; 7.F; 8.T; 9.F; 10.selectedIndex

# Practice

1. Modify Listing 1 so that each mouseup or mousedown will add 1 to a counter and the total displayed on the button.

2. Internet Explorer 4 supports the `onmouseover` and `onmouseout` events for a push button. Netscape Navigator 4.0 doesn't, but it may if you are using a later version. Write a script that will test these events. Each time the mouse is over the button, the caption should show a number that is 1 higher than the previous visit. When the mouse moves away from the button, the caption should say "Mouse Out."

3. Write a script to create 9 push button as shown in Figure 3.7.

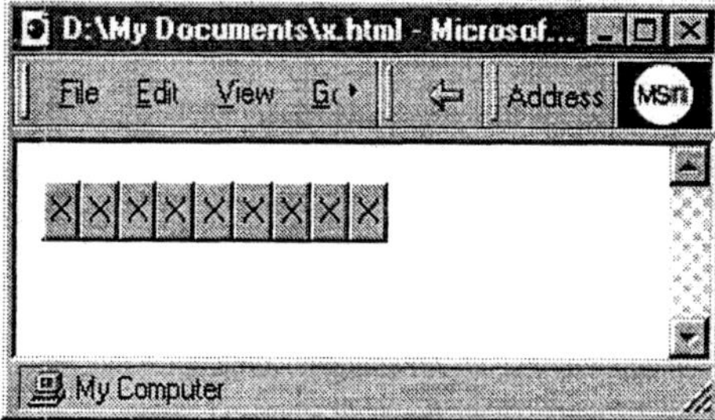


**Figure 3.7 Buttons created by a loop**

4. Modify the previous script to arrange the buttons in three rows, as shown in Figure 3.8.

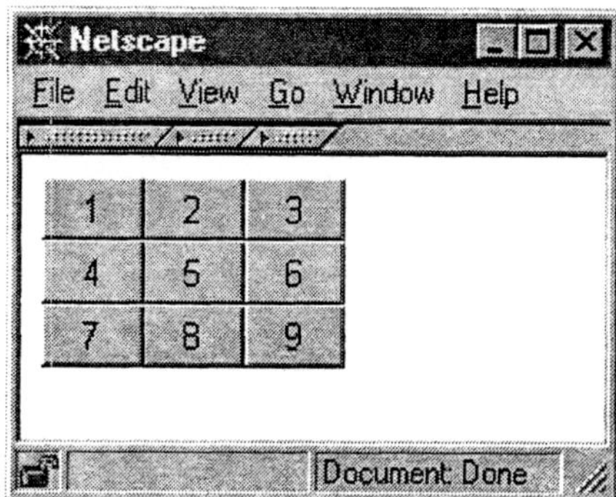


**Figure 3.8 Buttons in 3 columns and 3 rows**

5. Modify the previous script so that when a button is clicked, an alert box will show the number clicked.

6. In Listing 2, set the focus on the text box as soon as the document is loaded. What happens to the text box? Why?

7. How can you create a one-line text box whose value cannot be changed?

8. Create a five-row textarea box and use a script to fill in two columns of data as shown in Figure 3.9. Users should not be allowed to change the content in the box.

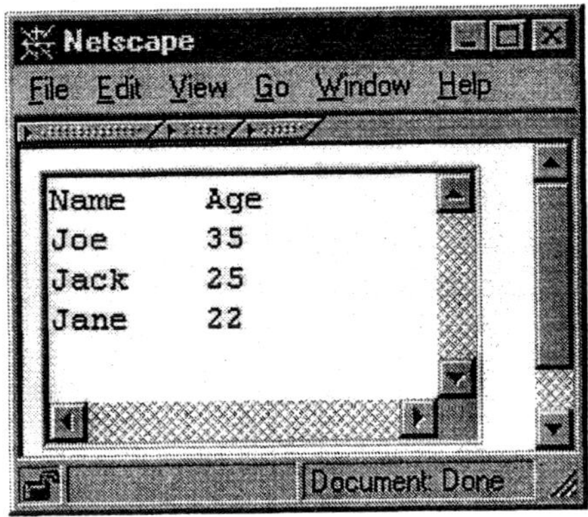


**Figure 3.9 A textarea box**

- 9. In Listing 3, use an if structure to prevent calculation if nothing is checked.

- 10. In Listing 3, modify the script to tabulate the total when the user checks or unchecks a checkbox. When a checkbox is checked, its value should be added. When it's unchecked, its value should be subtracted.

  The checkbox should be passed to the function, which should be able to handle float-point numbers (use the `parseFloat` function).

## Answers

1.

```
<HTML>
<HEAD>
<SCRIPT LANGUAGE="JavaScript">
<!--
 var counter = 0
 function mouseDown()
 {
   counter++
   document.forms[0].elements[0].value = counter
 }

 function mouseUp()
 {
```

```
    counter++
    document.forms[0].elements[0].value = counter
  }
//-->
</SCRIPT>
</HEAD>
<BODY>
<form>
<INPUT>
<INPUT TYPE="button" VALUE="Click To Increment"
onmousedown="mouseDown()" onmouseup="mouseUp()">
</form>
</BODY>
</HTML>
```

2.

```
<HTML>
<HEAD>
<SCRIPT LANGUAGE="JavaScript">
<!--
var num = 0
function countIt()
{
  document.forms[0].elements[0].value = "Count " + num++
}
//-->
</SCRIPT>
</HEAD>
<BODY>
<FORM>
<INPUT TYPE="button" VALUE="Mouse Over"
onmouseover="countIt()">
</FORM>
</BODY>
</HTML>
```

3.

```
<HTML>
<BODY>
<FORM>
<SCRIPT LANGUAGE="JavaScript">
<!--
 for (var i = 1; i <= 9; i++)
```

```
{
  document.write("<INPUT TYPE='button' WIDTH=40 VALUE='X'>")
}
//-->
</SCRIPT>
</FORM>
</BODY>
</HTML>
```

4.

```
<HTML>
<BODY>
<FORM>
<SCRIPT LANGUAGE="JavaScript">
<!--
 for (var i = 1; i <= 9; i++)
 {
   document.write("<INPUT TYPE='button' WIDTH=40 VALUE=" + i +">")
   if ((i % 3) == 0) document.write("<BR>")
 }
//-->
</SCRIPT>
</FORM>
</BODY>
</HTML>
```

5.

```
<HTML>
<HEAD>
<SCRIPT LANGUAGE="JavaScript">
<!--
 function checkIt(num)
 {alert("You clicked " + num)}
//-->
</SCRIPT>
</HEAD>
<BODY>
<FORM>
<SCRIPT LANGUAGE="JavaScript">
<!--
 for (var i = 1; i <= 9; i++)
 {
```

```
    document.write("<INPUT TYPE='button' WIDTH=40
onclick='checkIt(this.value)' VALUE=" + i + ">")
    if ((i % 3) == 0) document.write("<BR>")
  }
//-->
</SCRIPT>
</FORM>
</BODY>
</HTML>
```

6.
Add an event handler as shown below:

```
<BODY onload="document.myForm.txtHello.focus()">
```

This will automatically sets the focus on the text box. It will also trigger the onfocus event. So the text box immediately shows the "Hello" message.

7.
In Internet Explorer, you can add READONLY or DISABLED (no value) attribute to prevent user tinkering. These won't work with Netscape Navigator.

The following will work in both browsers:

```
<INPUT TYPE="text" NAME="text1" VALUE="XXX"
onchange="alert('You can\'t change this'); blur()">
```

If you change the content and press Enter, the alert box will show up. Then the original content will be restored.

8.

```
<HTML>
<BODY>
<FORM>
<TEXTAREA NAME="txtNames" ROWS=5
onfocus="blur()"></TEXTAREA>
<SCRIPT LANGUAGE="JavaScript">
<!--
 var names = ""
 names += "Name\tAge\n"
 names += "Joe\t35\n"
 names += "Jack\t25\n"
 names += "Jane\t22\n"
```

```
  document.forms[0].txtNames.value=names
//-->
</SCRIPT>
</FORM>
</BODY>
</HTML>
```

9.
add the following to just before the last line in the function:

```
if (sum == 0)
{
  alert ("You have to order something.")
  return
}
```

10.

```
<HTML>
<HEAD>
<SCRIPT LANGUAGE="JavaScript">
<!--
  var sum = 0

  function checkIt(box)
  {
    var entry = document.forms[0].txtOutput
      //the text box object

    if (box.checked)
      sum += parseFloat(box.value)
        //add up, convert value to float
    else
      sum -= parseFloat(box.value)
        //subtract
    entry.value = "Order total: $" + sum
  } //show total in text box
//-->
</SCRIPT>
</HEAD>
<BODY>
<FORM>
Check the items you wish to order:<BR>
<INPUT TYPE="checkbox" NAME="order" VALUE="10.09"
```

```
onclick="checkIt(this)">Pizza, $10.09<BR>
<INPUT TYPE="checkbox" NAME="order" VALUE="3.50"
onclick="checkIt(this)">Sandwich, $3.50<BR>
<INPUT TYPE="checkbox" NAME="order" VALUE="4.29"
onclick="checkIt(this)">Burger, $4.29<BR>
<INPUT TYPE="checkbox" NAME="order" VALUE="2.15"
onclick="checkIt(this)">Pie, $2.15<BR>
<INPUT NAME="txtOutput"><BR>
</FORM>
</BODY>
</HTML>
```

JavaScript * QuickStart

# <4> Fun Stuff

This chapter covers a mixed bag of materials. Most are quite fun to deal with, if you can get your scripts to work. Some are serious stuff. This chapter gives you a taste of some advanced programming you can do with JavaScript.

## The window Object

The **window** object is the top-level object and the container of all the other objects. The most common events include **onload** and **onunload**. These are used with the <BODY> tag to provide event handlers when the page is loaded or unloaded. This was demonstrated in Chapter 1.

The common methods include the following:

```
alert()
clearTimeout()
close()
confirm()
open()
prompt()
setTimeout()
```

The **open()** and **close()** methods are used to open and close a new window. This subject will be demonstrated shortly.

The **setTimeout()** and **clearTimeout()** methods are used to control a timer. The end of this chapter will cover them and other time-related issues.

We have repeatedly used **alert()**, **prompt()**, and **confirm()**. Most of time we use these methods alone. We could have used them like this:

```
window.alert("xxx")
x = window.prompt("Enter your name:", "")
```

```
yes = window.confirm("Do you want to quit?")
```

Since **window** is the default object, it can be omitted.

This object also has quite a few properties. The useful ones include **status** and **defaultStatus**. The text string assigned to **defaultStatus** is displayed in the status bar when the browser is not showing its own messages. The text string assigned to **status** is shown under some circumstances.

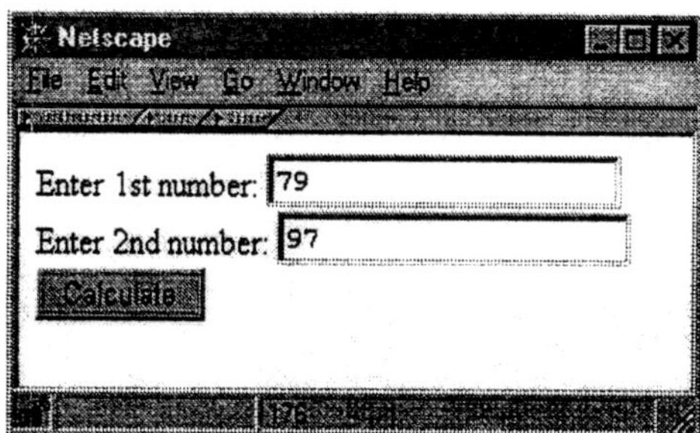


**Figure 4.1 Status bar message**

Here is an example. It produces Figure 4.1.

```
<HTML>
<HEAD>
<SCRIPT LANGUAGE="JavaScript">
<!--
  window.defaultStatus = "Add"
    //initial status string
  function calculate(form)
  {
    num1 = Number(form.text1.value)
    num2 = Number(form.text2.value)
    window.status = num1 + num2
  }  //show result in status bar
//-->
</SCRIPT>
</HEAD>
<BODY>
<FORM>
Enter 1st number:
<INPUT TYPE="text" NAME="text1"><BR>
Enter 2nd number:
<INPUT TYPE="text" NAME="text2"><BR>
<INPUT TYPE="button" VALUE="Calculate"
```

```
onclick="calculate(this.form)">
</FORM>
</BODY>
</HTML>
```

After this file is loaded, the "Add" string appears in the status bar. This is in the middle in Netscape Navigator. In Internet Explorer, this is the first box in the bottom left corner; it may not appear if the browser window is not big enough.

After you enter numbers in the two text boxes, clicking the Calculate button shows the sum in the status bar. But as you move the pointer away from the button, the default message reappears.

# The `document` Object

The **`document`** object, a child of the **`window`** object, is the equivalent of the <BODY> block. A number of attributes you normally set by using the <BODY> tag can also be manipulated with the **`document`** object. These include various links and colors, including the **`bgColor`**, which we'll cover in another section below.

The major child object of the **`document`** object is the **`form`** object. This was covered in Chapter 3.

These are the common methods:

```
open()
close()
write()
writeln()
```

You use these to open/close a document and write something to it.

The **`writeln()`** method does the same thing as **`write()`**, except adding a carriage return at the end. Keep in mind that this has no effect unless you use this method inside a <PRE> block.

The **`document.open()`** and **`document.close()`** methods are mostly used in conjunction with **`window.open()`** and **`window.close()`** to write to a new window. Both will be demonstrated below.

# Opening New Windows

Opening a new window follows this syntax:

```
winName = window.open(URL, targetName, "attributes")
```

If you want to reference this window, you need to give it a name. Such a name is not necessary if you don't want to programmatically reference it. You can specify a URL to load an existing page into this window. You can give this window a target name for the purpose of linking. The <A> and <FRAME> tags can then use this target name to load a page into this window. The last parameter lets you specify a series of attributes for this window.

The following statement opens an empty window with all the window accessories:

```
w = window.open("", "",
"resizable,menubar,scrollbars,status,titlebar,toolbar")
```

The whole statement should appear in a single line. Also, adding a space between two attributes may lead Netscape Navigator to ignore your command.

The following statements will open a new window and write a text string to it:

```
w = window.open("", "",
"resizable,menubar,scrollbars,status,titlebar,toolbar")
w.document.open()
w.document.write("Hello")
w.document.close()
```

Netscape Navigator will open a new window for the first time. When you try another time, it will reuse the same window.

Internet Explorer will open a new window each time. So you need to close them if you don't want to have too many windows to clutter your screen.

The **`document.open()`** and **`document.close()`** statements open and close the page for the purpose of writing to it (or loading an existing page). They don't affect the **`window`** object. Their absence does not affect Internet Explorer but will lead Netscape Navigator astray. Both browsers will work without **`document.open`**. But without **`document.close`** (or **`document.clear`**), Netscape Navigator will suspend itself and wait indefinitely for closing or clearing before doing any writing.

Notice that we precede **document** with the name of the new window. If the window name is omitted, writing will be done to the current (original) window.

You can also supply numbers (in pixels) to specify the height or width of the new window, as illustrated below.

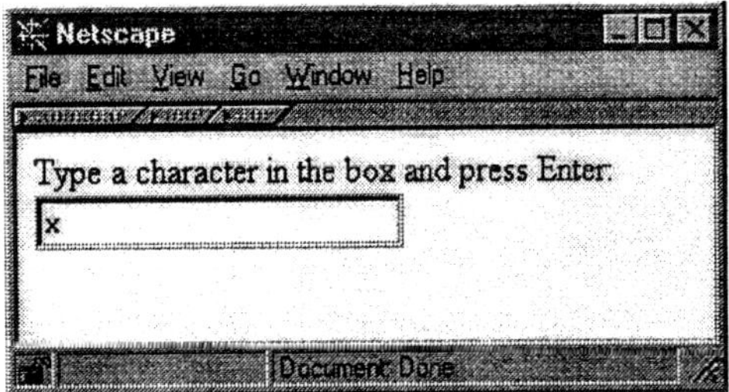


**Figure 4.2 Supplying a character**

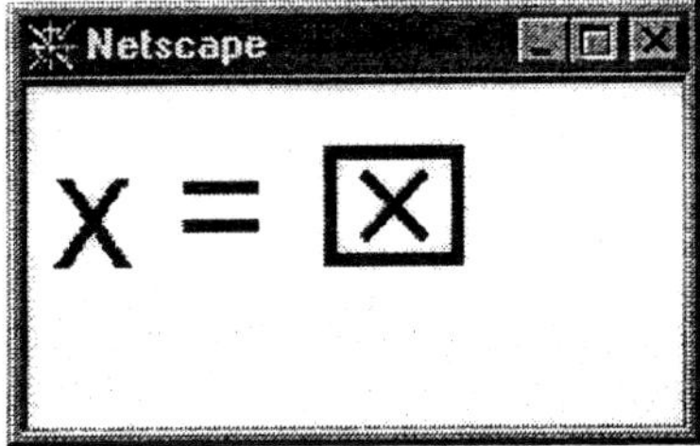


**Figure 4.3 Showing a Wingdings character**

Our source code below produces Figure 4.2. You can type a character in the text box and press Enter. A new window will open to display the equivalent Wingdings character, as shown in Figure 4.3.

```
<HTML>
<HEAD>
<SCRIPT LANGUAGE="JavaScript">
<!--
  function showChar(sign)
  {
    w = window.open("", "", "height=100,width=200")
    w.document.open()
```

```
    w.document.write("<FONT FACE='arial' COLOR='red'
SIZE=7>" + sign + " = ")
    w.document.write("<FONT FACE='wingdings' COLOR='red'
SIZE=7>" + sign)
    w.document.close()
  }
//-->
</SCRIPT>
</HEAD>
<BODY>
<FORM>
Type a character in the box and press Enter:<BR>
<INPUT TYPE="text" onchange="showChar(this.value)">
</FORM>
</BODY>
</HTML>
```

We can use an **idle loop** as a crude timer to automatically close the window after a while. Add the following to the end of the function:

```
    for (i = 0; i < 10000; i++)
      {}
    w.close()
```

Our **for** loop won't do anything except killing time. When the time is up, the window will automatically close. How long will such a loop last? It depends on your computer and the browser. Netscape Navigator will take much longer than Internet Explorer.

# Opening New Pages

What happens if you don't open a new window and just write text to the **document** object? That depends on when the writing is done. If you write before the document is loaded and displayed (closed), the output will become part of the current page. If you write after the page has been loaded, a new page will open up to display the output. The same window is used to display the new page. You can return to the previous page by clicking the browser's Back button.

The following source file uses an <A> (anchor) tag with the HREF (hypertext reference) attribute to create a link. Normally you use this arrangement to create a hyperlink and let users click the link to download a page to your browser. Instead of using HREF to specify a URL (such as http://www.microsoft.com), we use it to call a local function.

```
<HTML>
<HEAD>
<SCRIPT LANGUAGE="JavaScript">
<!--
  var i = 0
  function newpage()
  {
    i++  //works in IE, not in NN
    document.open()
    document.write("Hello, page " + i)
    document.close()
  }
//-->
</SCRIPT>
</HEAD>
<BODY>
<FORM>
<A HREF="javascript: void(newpage())">
Open a new page.</A>
</FORM>
</BODY>
</HTML>
```

This source file will create a single link ("Open a new page."). Clicking this link will activate this reference:

```
javascript: void(newpage())
```

This tells the browser to call a script function and return nothing. This can also be written like below (you can even remove the **void** keyword):

```
javascript: void newpage()
```

The following will also work in both browsers:

```
<A HREF="javascript:" onclick="newpage()">
Open a new page.</A>
```

Our function will open a new page and write one line to it. Internet Explorer will write "Hello, page 1" to this new page. The number is always 1 no matter how many times you click this link. Netscape Navigator will consider the variable undefined and give us an error. On the other hand, if the caller passes a number to the function, this number will be recognized by both browsers and written to the new page.

You can use the **location** property of the **document** object to load a new document to the current window. The following statement will load a file from the current directory:

```
document.location = "colors.html"
```

You can also use the **location** property of the **window** object. Anyone of the following will also work:

```
location = "url"
location.href = "url"
window.location.href = "url"
```

# Tracking Object Members

There is a **for-in** statement that can be used to loop through an object's components. It follows this syntax:

```
for (varX in objX)
  {statements}
```

It will go through all the properties (and events) of the object named objX and store it in the variable named varX.

The two browsers produce quite different results. Internet Explorer will count all the events and properties (but not methods). Netscape Navigator will count only properties and nothing else. Netscape Navigator will count global variables as properties, but Internet Explorer won't.

If you want to know how many members come with your browser's **window** object, try this loop:

```
for (i in window)
  alert(i)
```

You can also show lower-level objects by trying one of the following:

```
for (i in window.document)
  {...}
for (i in window.document.forms[0])
  {...}
for (i in window.document.forms[0].elements[0])
  {...}
```

The last two assume that you have a form and a control in the current page.

If you have both browsers, you might want to test these statements on both of them. You'll find quite a few differences showing how different the two browsers implement the DOM.

# Colors

You can set many colors for multiple parts of a Web page. Chapter 1 tells you how to use the COLOR attribute with the <FONT> tag to mark up a block of text. You can also use the BGCOLOR attribute with the <BODY> tag or table-related tags (see another section below) to set background colors.

A color value can be a common English word such as red, green, blue, brown, etc. There are numerous valid words. If you don't know whether a name is a valid color value, try it to see whether it works. If a browser doesn't recognize the word, no change is made.

A color value can also be specified with the RGB (red, green, blue) values. Each specific component can be from 00 to FF (hex value for 255). So <FONT COLOR="#ff0000">xxx</FONT> (the # sign is optional) will mark up the text with red color. You can mix these components with various amounts to produce numerous results.

Normally, a background color is set in the <BODY> tag and cannot be changed after the document is loaded. However, the `document.bgColor` property can be manipulated by a script to change the background color. You can also use the `document.fgColor` property to set text color before using `write()` to output text in that color.

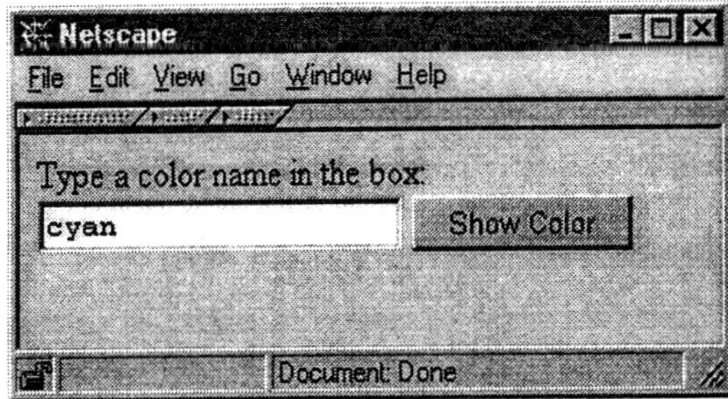


**Figure 4.4 Showing a background color**

The following code will produce Figure 4.4. You can enter a color value in the text box and click the Show button to change the background color. A color value can be in a valid word or a hex number. So "yellow" and "#ffff00" will produce the same result.

```
<HTML>
<HEAD>
<SCRIPT LANGUAGE="JavaScript">
<!--
  function show(color)
  {
    document.bgColor = color
  }
//-->
</SCRIPT>
</HEAD>
<BODY>
<FORM>
<!-- no form name is required here -->
Type a color name in the box:<BR>
<INPUT TYPE="text" NAME="txtColor">
<INPUT TYPE="button" VALUE="Show Color"
onClick="show(txtColor.value)">
</FORM>
</BODY>
</HTML>
```

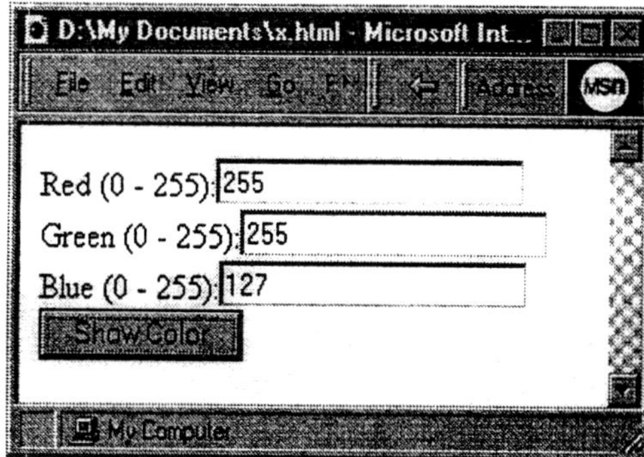


**Figure 4.5 Supplying RGB values**

Our next example (Figure 4.5) lets the user enter the RGB values in decimal numbers:

```
<HTML>
<HEAD>
```

```
<SCRIPT LANGUAGE="JavaScript">
<!--
function show(r, g, b)
{
  r = Number(r)    //convert to numeric
  g = Number(g)
  b = Number(b)
  r = r.toString(16)    //convert to hex
  g = g.toString(16)
  b = b.toString(16)
  document.bgColor = r + g + b
}
//-->
</SCRIPT>
</HEAD>
<BODY>
<FORM>
Red (0 - 255):<INPUT TYPE="text" NAME="R"><BR>
Green (0 - 255):<INPUT TYPE="text" NAME="G"><BR>
Blue (0 - 255):<INPUT TYPE="text" NAME="B"><BR>
<INPUT TYPE="button" VALUE="Show Color"
onClick="show(R.value, G.value, B.value)">
</FORM>
</BODY>
</HTML>
```

Since a number entered into a text box is a text string, we need to use the **Number** function to convert it to a numeric so that it can be arithmetically manipulated.

The **toString** function converts a base-10 (decimal) numeric to another number of a specified base. For example, the following statements will produce the numbers shown in the comments:

```
var x = 123
alert(x.toString(2))        //1111011
alert(x.toString(8))        //173
alert(x.toString(16))       //7b
```

The above returned numbers are **binary** (base-2), **octal** (base-8), and **hexadecimal** (base-16). You can use any base number with this function.

# Tables

You can use a series of tags to create tables with or without borders, with different border colors, and with different background colors or images.

A table starts with <TABLE> and ends with </TABLE>. This container in turn contains a series of rows created with the <TR> tag. A row container, in turn, can contain a series of cells created with <TD>. If you want a header, use <TH> instead of <TD>. You can optionally add a caption with the <CAPTION> tag.

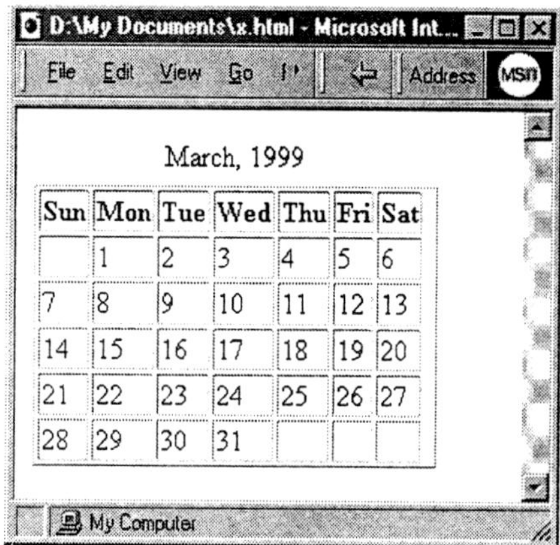


March, 1999

| Sun | Mon | Tue | Wed | Thu | Fri | Sat |
|---|---|---|---|---|---|---|
| | 1 | 2 | 3 | 4 | 5 | 6 |
| 7 | 8 | 9 | 10 | 11 | 12 | 13 |
| 14 | 15 | 16 | 17 | 18 | 19 | 20 |
| 21 | 22 | 23 | 24 | 25 | 26 | 27 |
| 28 | 29 | 30 | 31 | | | |

**Figure 4.6 Table demo**

The following source file creates the table shown in Figure 4.6.

```
<HTML>
<BODY>
<TABLE BORDER=1>  <!--1 pixel for border-->
<CAPTION>March, 1999</CAPTION>
<TR>
  <TH>Sun<TH>Mon<TH>Tue<TH>Wed<TH>Thu<TH>Fri<TH>Sat
  <TH>
<TR>
  <TD><BR><TD>1<TD>2<TD>3<TD>4<TD>5<TD>6
<TR>
  <TD>7<TD>8<TD>9<TD>10<TD>11<TD>12<TD>13
<TR>
  <TD>14<TD>15<TD>16<TD>17<TD>18<TD>19<TD>20
<TR>
  <TD>21<TD>22<TD>23<TD>24<TD>25<TD>26<TD>27
<TR>
  <TD>28<TD>29<TD>30<TD>31<TD><BR><TD><BR><TD>
  <BR>
</TABLE>
</BODY>
</HTML>
```

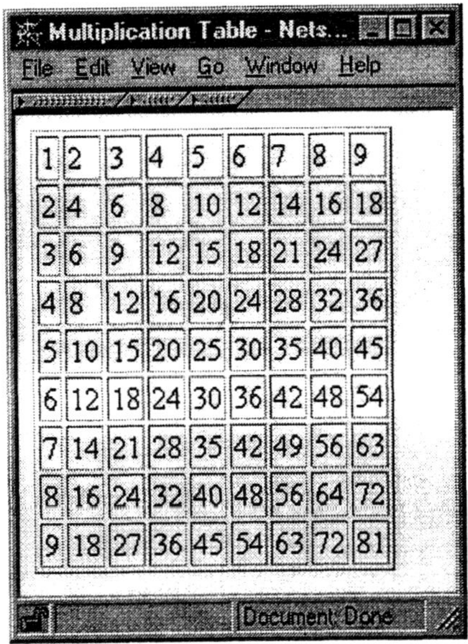


| 1 | 2 | 3 | 4 | 5 | 6 | 7 | 8 | 9 |
|---|---|---|---|---|---|---|---|---|
| 2 | 4 | 6 | 8 | 10 | 12 | 14 | 16 | 18 |
| 3 | 6 | 9 | 12 | 15 | 18 | 21 | 24 | 27 |
| 4 | 8 | 12 | 16 | 20 | 24 | 28 | 32 | 36 |
| 5 | 10 | 15 | 20 | 25 | 30 | 35 | 40 | 45 |
| 6 | 12 | 18 | 24 | 30 | 36 | 42 | 48 | 54 |
| 7 | 14 | 21 | 28 | 35 | 42 | 49 | 56 | 63 |
| 8 | 16 | 24 | 32 | 40 | 48 | 56 | 64 | 72 |
| 9 | 18 | 27 | 36 | 45 | 54 | 63 | 72 | 81 |

**Figure 4.7  A table created by a script**

The chore of creating tables can be automated with scripts. The following source code creates the table shown in Figure 4.7.

```
<HTML>    <!--table.html-->
<HEAD>
<TITLE>
Multiplication Table
</TITLE>
</HEAD>
<BODY>
<SCRIPT LANGUAGE="JavaScript">
<!--
    var i, j
    document.write("<TABLE BORDER=1>")
    for(i = 1; i <= 9; i++)
    {
       document.write("<TR>");     //9 rows
       for(j = 1; j <= 9; j++)
       {
         document.write("<TD>")
         document.write(i * j)
         document.write("</TD>")
           /* 9 columns for each row
              create col and fill in number */
```

```
            }
            document.write("</TR>")
        }
        document.write("</TABLE>")
//-->
</SCRIPT>
</BODY>
</HTML>
```

# Arrays

An array is a variable that contains multiple individual variables. Each individual variable is distinguished from another by an index (subscript) number. The index number starts from 0. So the first element (member) has the index value of 0.

JavaScript has no array data type. But you can create an array object, like this:

```
var arrX = new Array()
```

As usual, the **var** keyword is optional. After this statement, arrX is recognized as an array object.

You can specify a limit by supplying the highest index number, like this:

```
var arrX = new Array(5)
```

This array can have up to 6 members, which are indexed from 0 to 5. Without this limit, an array can store any number of members.

After an array is created, you need to populate it by assigning values to individual members.

```
var names = new Array(2)
names[0] = "Jim"
names[1] = "Kim"
names[2] = "Tim"
```

You can create and populate an array at the same time. The single statement below will do the same thing as the above four statements:

```
var names = new Array("Jim", "Kim", "Tim")
```

Notice that parameters are enclosed in parentheses, such as (2). But an array index is enclosed in a pair of square brackets, such as [0].

Once an array is populated, you can use a loop or some other ways to manipulate the members. The following loop will show each individual name in an alert box:

```
for (var i = 0; i <= names.length-1; i++)
   {alert(names[i])}
```

The **`length`** property of an array can tell you the total number of members in the array. This number is one higher than the highest index value because the index starts with 0. So in a loop, you need to subtract 1 from this value to get the highest index value.

You can assign **`new Array()`** to a member of an array to create another array within an existing array. This allows you to manipulate **multidimensional arrays**. Before we demonstrate that, we'll first create a table with the following source file:

```
<HTML>
<BODY>
<TABLE BORDER>
<CAPTION>
<B>Grade Report</B>
</CAPTION>
<TR>
    <TH ROWSPAN=2 VALIGN="bottom">Name
    <TH COLSPAN=3>Test
    <TH ROWSPAN=2 VALIGN="bottom">Grade
<TR>
    <TD WIDTH=25>1<TD WIDTH=25>2<TD WIDTH=25>3
<TR>
    <TD>Adams<TD>89<TD>86<TD>87<TD ALIGN="center">B
<TR>
    <TD>Johnson<TD>92<TD>89<TD>93<TD ALIGN="center">A
<TR>
    <TD>Smith<TD>79<TD>76<TD>77<TD ALIGN="center">C
</TABLE>
</BODY>
</HTML>
```

Figure 4.8 shows the result. Here we use the COLSPAN and ROWSPAN attributes to specify how many columns or rows an entry is supposed to span. These attributes can also be used with the <TD> tag.

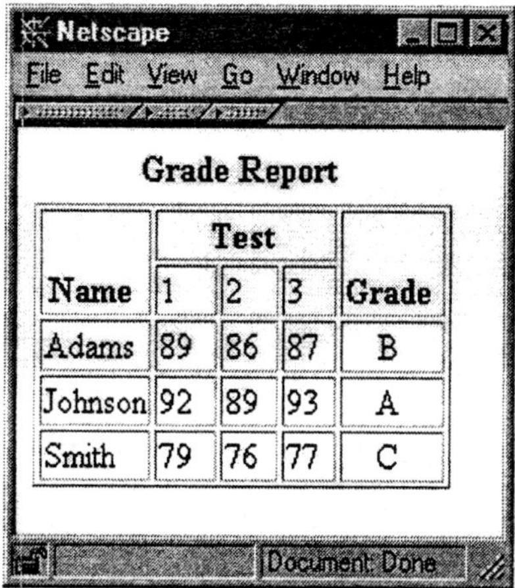


**Figure 4.8 Cells spanning across rows and columns**

We can use a multidimensional array to manipulate the test scores, like this:

```
<HTML>       <!--grades1.html-->
<BODY>
<TABLE BORDER>
<CAPTION>
<B>Grade Report</B>
</CAPTION>
<TR>
    <TH ROWSPAN=2 VALIGN="bottom">Name
    <TH COLSPAN=3>Test
    <TH ROWSPAN=2 VALIGN="bottom">Grade
<TR>
    <TD WIDTH=25>1<TD WIDTH=25>2<TD WIDTH=25>3
<SCRIPT LANGUAGE="JavaScript">
<!--
  var students = new Array()
  students[0] = new Array()
  students[1] = new Array()
  students[2] = new Array()

  var i, j, grade

  students[0][0] = "Adams"
  students[0][1] = 89
  students[0][2] = 86
  students[0][3] = 87

  students[1][0] = "Johnson"
```

```
  students[1][1] = 92
  students[1][2] = 89
  students[1][3] = 93

  students[2][0] = "Smith"
  students[2][1] = 79
  students[2][2] = 76
  students[2][3] = 77

  for (i = 0; i <= 2; i++)
  {
    document.write ("<TR>")          //create row
    document.write ("<TD>")          //create cell
    document.write (students[i][0])  //write name
    grade = null;   //clear var for reuse

    for (j = 1; j <=3; j++)
    {
      grade += students[i][j];  //add up scores
      document.write ("<TD>");          //create cell
      document.write (students[i][j]); //write score
    }

    if (grade >= 270) grade = "A"
    if (grade >= 240) grade = "B"
    if (grade >= 210) grade = "C"
    if (grade >= 180) grade = "D"
    if (grade < 180) grade = "F"

    document.write ("<TD ALIGN='center'>")
    document.write (grade)
  }
//-->
</SCRIPT>
</TABLE>
</BODY>
</HTML>
```

This will produce the same output as before, except that the grades are determined by the script.

If you want everything to be done in script, do it this way:

```
<HTML>      <!--grades2.html-->
<BODY>
<SCRIPT LANGUAGE="JavaScript">
<!--
  var students = new Array()
  students[0] = new Array()
  students[1] = new Array()
```

```
    students[2] = new Array()

    var i, j, grade

    document.write ("<TABLE BORDER>")
    document.write ("<CAPTION>")
    document.write ("<B>Grade Report</B>")
    document.write ("</CAPTION>")
    document.write ("<TR>")
    document.write ("<TH ROWSPAN=2 VALIGN='bottom'>Name")
    document.write ("<TH COLSPAN=3>Test")
    document.write ("<TH ROWSPAN=2 VALIGN='bottom'>Grade")
    document.write ("<TR>")
    document.write ("<TD WIDTH=25>1<TD WIDTH=25>2<TD
WIDTH=25>3")

    students[0][0] = "Adams"
    students[0][1] = 79
    students[0][2] = 86
    students[0][3] = 82

    students[1][0] = "Johnson"
    students[1][1] = 92
    students[1][2] = 89
    students[1][3] = 93

    students[2][0] = "Smith"
    students[2][1] = 79
    students[2][2] = 76
    students[2][3] = 77

    for (i = 0; i <=2; i++)
    {
      document.write ("<TR>")          //create row
      document.write ("<TD>")          //create cell
      document.write (students[i][0])  //write name
      grade = null;   //clear var for reuse

      for (j = 1; j <=3; j++)
      {
        grade += students[i][j]  //add up scores
        document.write ("<TD>")           //create cell
        document.write (students[i][j]) //write score
      }

      if (grade >= 270) grade = "A"
      if (grade >= 240) grade = "B"
      if (grade >= 210) grade = "C"
      if (grade >= 180) grade = "D"
      if (grade < 180) grade = "F"
```

```
        document.write ("<TD ALIGN='center'>")
        document.write (grade)
    }
//-->
</SCRIPT>
</TABLE>
</BODY>
</HTML>
```

# Point and Click Calculator

This section creates a point-and-click calculator, as shown in Figure 4.9. You can click each displayed character to enter it into the same box. Clicking the Calculate button will show the result. Clicking the Clear button will clear any entries in the two text boxes.

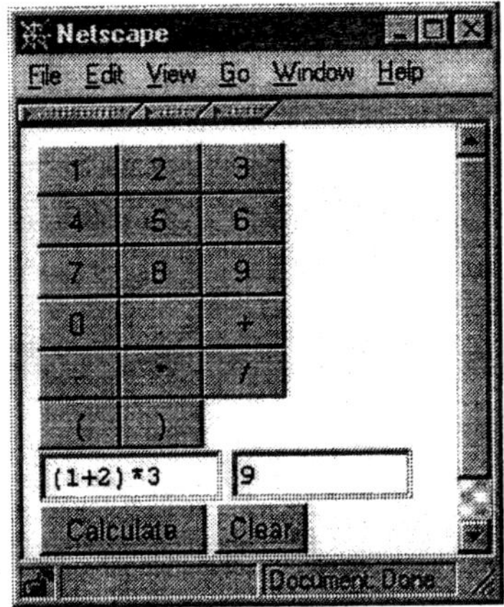


**Figure 4.9 A calculator**

The source code shown below uses two **for** loops to simplify the chore of creating the buttons. A one-dimensional array is also used for this purpose. Without these techniques, you'll need to enter lengthy HTML codes to create this display.

```
<HTML>        <!--calculator.html-->
<HEAD>
<SCRIPT LANGUAGE="JavaScript">
<!--
  var nums = ""
```

```
    //global variable
  function combine(num)
  {
    nums += num   //concatenate digits
    document.form1.txtInput.value = nums
      //show in the first text box
      //form is not passed
  }
  function calcIt(form)
  {
    form.txtOutput.value = eval(form.txtInput.value)
      //evaluate and output to 2nd box
      //form is passed
  }
//-->
</SCRIPT>
</HEAD>
<BODY>
<FORM NAME="form1">
<SCRIPT LANGUAGE="JavaScript">
<!--
  var i
  for (i = 1; i <= 9; i++)
  {
    document.write("<INPUT TYPE='button' VALUE=" +
    i + " WIDTH=40 onclick='combine(this.value)'>")
    if ((i % 3) == 0)
      {document.write("<BR>")}
      //add break after every 3
  }

  var signs = new Array(7)
    //create a new array with 8 elements
    //length is 8, last index is 7
  signs[0] = "0"
  signs[1] = "."
  signs[2] = "+"
  signs[3] = "-"
  signs[4] = "*"
  signs[5] = "/"
  signs[6] = "("
  signs[7] = ")"

  for (i = 0; i <= signs.length-1; i++)
  {
    document.write("<INPUT TYPE='button' VALUE=" +
    signs[i] + " WIDTH=40 onclick='combine(this.value)'>")
    if (((i + 1) % 3) == 0)
      {document.write("<BR>")}
  }
  document.write("<BR>")       //last break
```

```
//-->
</SCRIPT>

<INPUT TYPE="text" SIZE=10 NAME="txtInput">
<INPUT TYPE="text" SIZE=10 NAME="txtOutput"><BR>
<INPUT TYPE="button" VALUE="Calculate"
onclick="calcIt(this.form)">
<INPUT TYPE="reset" VALUE="Clear" onclick="nums=''">
  <!--reset global variable on click-->
</FORM>
</BODY>
</HTML>
```

# Date and Time Manipulation

JavaScript comes with a number of built-in objects and functions to let you manipulate date and time items. You can use them to create a timer display or a digital clock.

## Timer

There is a built-in timer that is a method of the **window** object. This method's name is **setTimeout()**. You can give it two arguments, the first to do something and the second to set an interval. It follows this syntax:

```
id = window.setTimeout("instruction", interval)
```

As usual, the **window** reference is optional because it's the default. The optional **id** variable is a name to identify this method for later use by other functions. The instruction can be some statements such as calling itself (if you want a **recursion**) or another function.

The interval value is based on milliseconds (one thousandth of a second), so 1000 will mean one second.

This timer activates itself at the specified interval. It works similar to the Timer control available in many packages such as Visual Basic. When the following statement is executed, it won't do anything and the computer continues to do other things. Three seconds later, however, an alert box will pop up by itself once.

```
setTimeout("alert('Hello')",3000)
```

**Figure 4.10 A timer display**

The following example produces the display shown in Figure 4.10. Every second, a new number appears in the text box. You can click Stop to stop the change. You can click Go to resume where you left off. You can also click Restart to start from the beginning.

```
<HTML>    <!--timer.html-->
<HEAD>
<SCRIPT LANGUAGE="JavaScript">
<!--
  var i = 0, id
  function showtime()
  {
    i++
    document.f1.text1.value = i + " seconds"
    id = setTimeout("showtime()", 1000)
  }

  function clearIt()
  {
    clearTimeout(id)
  }
//-->
</SCRIPT>
</HEAD>

<BODY onload = "showtime()">
<FORM NAME="f1">
<INPUT TYPE="text" NAME="text1"><BR>
<INPUT TYPE="button" VALUE="Stop"
onclick="clearIt()">
<INPUT TYPE="button" VALUE="Go"
onclick="clearIt(); showtime()">
```

```
<INPUT TYPE="reset" VALUE="Restart"
onclick="clearIt(); i=0; showtime()">
</FORM>
</BODY>
</HTML>
```

After this file is loaded, the **showtime()** function is automatically run because it's triggered by the **onload** event of the <BODY> tag.

The **setTimeout** method triggers itself at the interval of 1000 milliseconds. When that happens, the **showtime()** function is called again (this is an example of **recursion**). That will then change the display in the text box.

When the Stop button is clicked, the inline code invokes the **clearTimeout()** method to disable the timer named **id**, the name we've previously given to our timer.

When the Go button is clicked, we clear the previous timer and run it again. If the timer is not cleared first, you'll start another copy and the result will be inaccurate.

When the Restart button is clicked, we do the above and reset the global value as well. This will let us start from 0.

In our code, we place **clearTimeout()** in a function. This will work in both browsers. In Netscape Navigator, you can use inline code, such as this:

```
<INPUT TYPE="button" VALUE="Stop"
onclick="clearTimeout(id)">
```

But Internet Explorer will refuse to respond to this.

## Scrolling Text

It's fun to make a text string scroll continuously. In Internet Explorer, you can do it with <MARQUEE>xxx</MARQUEE>; the text between the two tags will continuously scroll from the right side of the browser window to the left. But Netscape Navigator won't respond to this tag.

You can use a timer and string manipulation to make a message scroll. Here is an example. The result is shown in Figure 4.11.

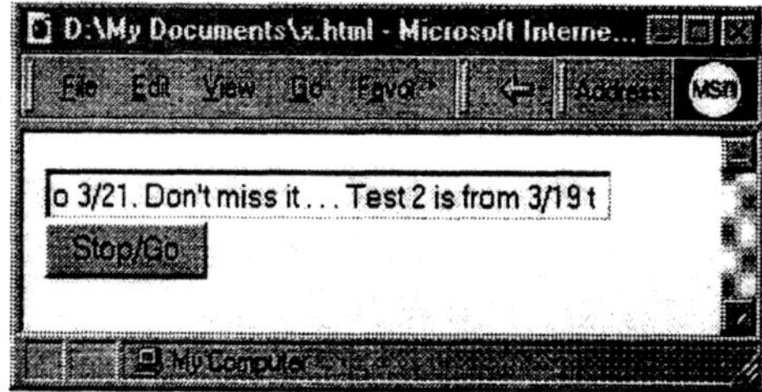


**Figure 4.11 Scrolling text**

```
<HTML>    <!--scroll.html-->
<HEAD>
<SCRIPT LANGUAGE="JavaScript">
<!--
  var msg = "Test 2 is 3/19 -- 3/21. Don't miss it . . . "
  var stop = false;    //to control stop or go
  var interval = 200
    //timer interval is 1/5 second
  var timerID;  //ID to control timer

  function showit()
  {
    document.f1.text1.value = msg
    msg = msg.substring(1, msg.length) +
    msg.substring(0, 1)
      //move each 1st char to back of string
    timerID = setTimeout("showit()", interval)
  }

  function stoporgo()
  {
    stop = !stop //rotate between true and false
    if (stop)    //if true
      {clearTimeout(timerID)}   //stop timer
    else                       //if not
      {
      showit()              //call function to resume
      }
  }
//-->
</SCRIPT>
</HEAD>

<BODY onload = "showit()">
<FORM NAME="f1">
<INPUT TYPE="text" NAME="text1" SIZE=35>
<INPUT TYPE="button" NAME="stopgo" VALUE="Stop/Go"
```

```
onclick="stoporgo()">
<BR>
</FORM>
</BODY>
</HTML>
```

We use the **substring()** function to extract the first letter and attach it to the end at the interval of every 1/5 (200/1000) second. The first argument in this function is the starting number and the second is the length value.

We use the **stop** variable to control the stop or go mechanism. It starts with the Boolean **false** value. When the Stop/Go button is clicked, the Not (!) operator changes it to **true**. That leads to the execution of **clearTimeout** to stop the scrolling. When the button is clicked again, the **false** value is restored and the **showit()** function is run again to activate the timer.

You may find a practical use for such a script. I maintain a Web site to teach a Web-based class. When a test is near, I'll add the above scrolling message to the home page, reminding students not to miss the test. It's hard to ignore an object when it's continuously moving.

## The Date Object

The **Date** object is useful to manipulate date and time data. You create a new date object with **new Date()** the same way as you create a new array object, as shown earlier. Here is an example:

```
var currDate = new Date()
```

After that, **currDate** becomes a date object. This object automatically stores the current date and time data. You can use the following methods to extract the needed data:

| | |
|---|---|
| getDate() | 1 - 31, day of the month |
| getDay() | 0 - 6, day of the week |
| getHours() | 0 - 23, current hour |
| getMinutes() | 0 - 59, current minute |
| getMonth() | 0 - 11, current month |
| getSeconds() | 0 - 59, current second |
| getTime() | milliseconds after 12/31/1969 |
| getYear() | number of years since 1900 |

Notice that **getDate()** is 1-based and the others are 0-based.

Following Java, JavaScript uses the beginning of 1970 as the base for date calculation. So **getTime()** returns the number of milliseconds since then. If you divide that by 365*24*60*60*1000, you'll get the approximate number of years since then. For example, if you get 29, it means 1999, or 29 years since 1970.

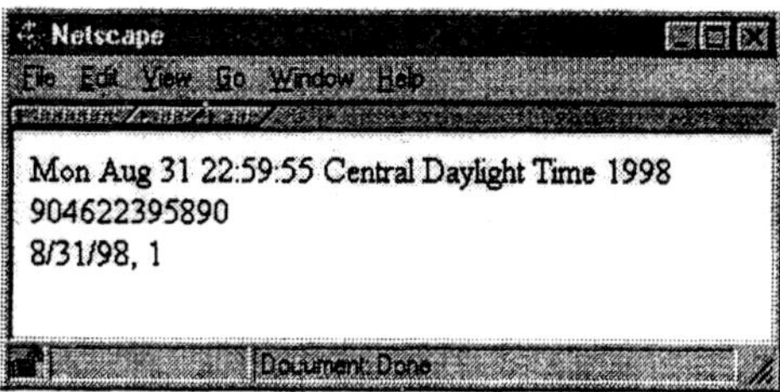


**Figure 4.12 Date and time information**

The following script produces the result shown in Figure 4.12. The comments in the source code tell you what each method is supposed to do.

```
<HTML>
<BODY>
<SCRIPT LANGUAGE="JavaScript">
<!--
  var temp = ""
  var currDate = new Date()
  document.write(currDate + "<BR>")
    //all date/time data
  var currTime = currDate.getTime()
    //milliseconds since 1/1/1970
  document.write(currTime + "<BR>")
  var mn = currDate.getMonth()
    //month 0 - 11
  temp += ++mn + "/"
    //add 1 to month number
  var mnDay = currDate.getDate()
    //day of month 1 - 31
  temp += mnDay + "/"
  var yr = currDate.getYear()
    //year number since 1990
  temp += yr + ", "
  document.write(temp)
  var wkDay = currDate.getDay()
    //day of week, 0 - 6
  document.write(wkDay)
```

```
//-->
</SCRIPT>
</BODY>
</HTML>
```

## Digital Clock

You can use some of the date object's methods to extract the current hour, minute, and second. Combining these with the **`setTimeout()`** function discussed earlier, you can create a digital clock. The source code is shown below. The result is shown in Figure 4.13.

```
<HTML>    <!--clock.html-->
<HEAD>
<SCRIPT LANGUAGE="JavaScript">
<!--
  function showtime()
  {
    var date1 = new Date()
      //create a date object
    var temp = "Current time = "
    var hr = date1.getHours()
      //get current hour from date object
    temp += hr + ":"
      //concatenate string
    var min = date1.getMinutes()
    temp += min + ":"
    var sec = date1.getSeconds()
    temp += sec

    document.f1.text1.value = temp
    var id = setTimeout("showtime()", 1000)
  }
//-->
</SCRIPT>
</HEAD>
<BODY onload = "showtime()">
<FORM NAME="f1">
<INPUT TYPE="text" NAME="text1" SIZE=25><BR>
</BODY>
</HTML>
```

For every method starting with *get* there is another one starting with *set*, such as **`setYear`**. You can use these to give properties to a date object. You can use this mechanism to create a perpetual calendar. It's too long to be put here. If you are interested, see *The JavaScript Coursebook.*

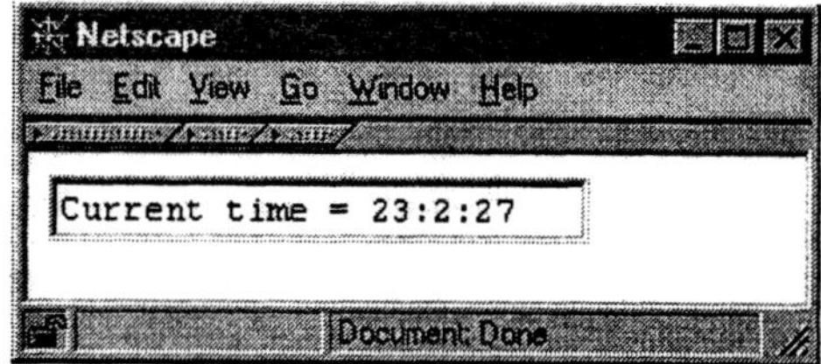


**Figure 4.13 A digital clock**

# Drill

____ 1. <A ______ = "javascript: void(func())"> calls a local function.

____ 2. The onload event is a member of this object:
- a. window
- b. document
- c. form
- d. control

____ 3. "location" is a property of:
- a. window
- b. document
- c. form
- d. both a and b
- e. none of the above

____ 4. "open()" opens a new document. True or false?

____ 5. _______ = "xxx" sends a text string to the browser's bottom panel.

____ 6. The following alert box will show ______ .

```
x = 2
alert(x.toString(2))
```

____ 7. The following statement will show the current date in the status bar. True of false?

```
<BODY onload="defaultStatus = new Date()">
```

____ 8. The following statement will cause an error because it is attempting to write an object. True of false?

```
document.write(new Date())
```

____ 9. The following alert box will show:

```
alert("democracy".substring(0, 4))
```

a. "dem"
b. "demo"
c. "democracy"
d. none of the above

____ 10. The following alert box will show _____ .

```
var arrX = new Array(6)
alert(arrX.length)
```

ANSWERS: 1.HREF; 2.a; 3.d; 4.F; 5.status; 6.10; 7.T; 8.F; 9.b; 10.6

# Practice

1. Write a script that uses a **for-in** loop to loop through all the members of the **window** object and writes the resulting member names to the window in a single column, one line for each name.

2. Modify the previous script to write all the members of the **document** object. Also keep track of the count and output it at the end.

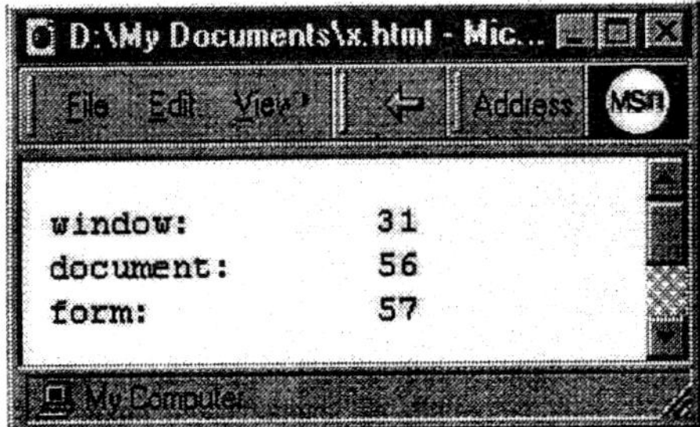


**Figure 4.14 Counting form properties**

3. Modify the previous script to count the members of the window, document, and form objects. Write the counts to the window in three separate lines with two columns, as shown in Figure 4.14.

4. Write a script that will convert a decimal number to a number of another base. As shown in Figure 4.15 , you can enter a number in the first text box and a base number in the second. Clicking the Show Output button should display an alert box showing the result.

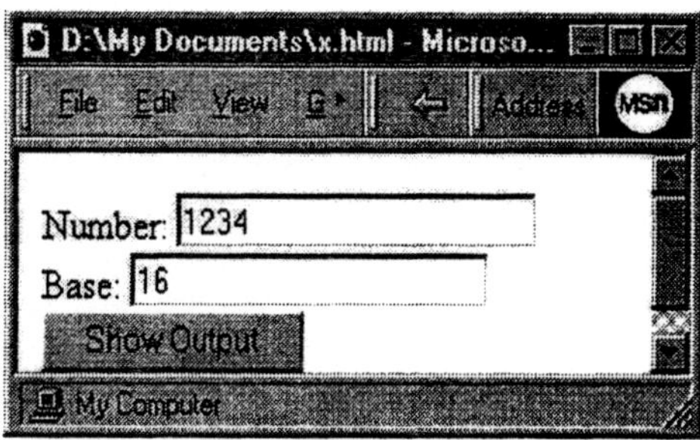


**Figure 4.15 Converting a number**

5. Write a script that will do the following:

   a. Open a new window and write a text string to it.
   b. Start a count-down timer from 10 to 0 and show in the status bar each number at a one-second interval.
   c. Close the window after 10 seconds.

6. Explain what the following script will do.

```
<HTML>
<HEAD>
</HEAD>
<BODY>
<FORM>
<SCRIPT LANGUAGE="JavaScript">
<!--
 with (window.document)
   for (i in forms[0])
     write(i + " ")
//-->
</SCRIPT>
```

```
</FORM>
</BODY>
</HTML>
```

7. Explain what the following script will do.

```
<HTML>
<HEAD>
</HEAD>
<BODY>
<FORM>
<SCRIPT LANGUAGE="JavaScript">
<!--
 with (window.document)
 {
   fgColor = "#ff0000"
   bgColor = "#ffff00"
   write("<H1 ALIGN=\"center\">Hello</H1>")
 }
//-->
</SCRIPT>
</FORM>
</BODY>
</HTML>
```

8. Write a script to output four columns as shown in Figure 4.16. The first column should be decimal numbers from 10 to 30. The other columns should display the first column's corresponding values in binary, octal, and hex formats.

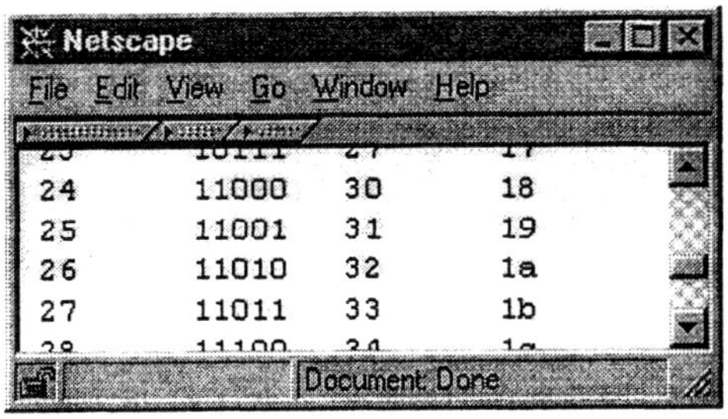

**Figure 4.16 Converting numbers**

9. Modify the previous script so that there is a text box for the user to enter a decimal number. When the Enter key is pressed, an alert box will show the equivalent binary, octal, and hex numbers as shown in Figure 4.17.

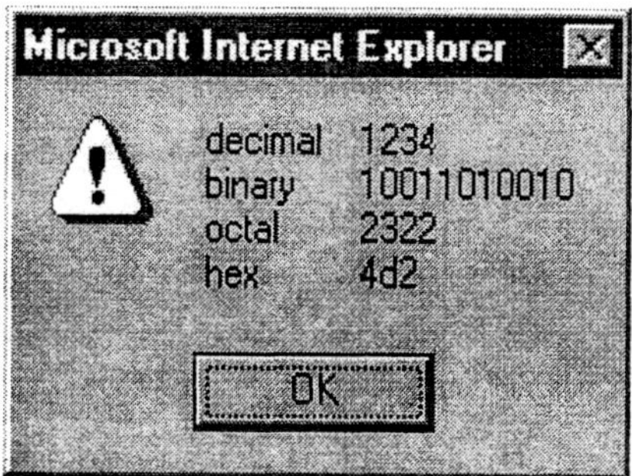


**Figure 4.17 Converted numbers**

10. Write a function that will show in the status bar the elapsed time in minutes and seconds. The function should start as soon as the page is loaded. The function should call itself to update the timer every second.

## Answers

1.

```
<HTML>
<BODY>
<SCRIPT LANGUAGE="JavaScript">
<!--
 var i, x = ""
 for (i in window)
   {x += i + "\n"}
 document.write("<PRE>")
 document.write(x)
//-->
</SCRIPT>
</BODY>
</HTML>
```

2.

```
<SCRIPT LANGUAGE="JavaScript">
```

```
<!--
 var i, x = "", count = 0
 for (i in document)
   {x += i + "\n"; count++}
 document.write("<PRE>")
 document.write(x)
 document.write(count)
//-->
```

3.

```
<HTML>
<BODY>
<FORM>
<SCRIPT LANGUAGE="JavaScript">
<!--
 var i
 var wincount = 0
 var doccount = 0
 var frmcount = 0

 for (i in window)
   {wincount++}

 for (i in document)
   {doccount++}

 for (i in document.forms[0])
   {frmcount++}

 document.write("<PRE>")
 document.write("window: " + "\t" + wincount + "\n")
 document.write("document: " + "\t" + doccount + "\n")
 document.write("form: " + "\t\t" + frmcount)
//-->
</SCRIPT>
</FORM>
</BODY>
</HTML>
```

4.

```
<HTML>
<HEAD>
<SCRIPT LANGUAGE="JavaScript">
```

```
<!--
function show(num, base)
{
  num = Number(num)   //convert to numeric
  base = Number(base)
  alert(num.toString(base))
}
//-->
</SCRIPT>
</HEAD>
<BODY>
<FORM>
Number: <INPUT TYPE="text" NAME="txtNum"> <BR>
Base: <INPUT TYPE="text" NAME="txtBase"> <BR>
<INPUT TYPE="button" VALUE="Show Output"
onClick="show(txtNum.value, txtBase.value)">
</FORM>
</BODY>
</HTML>
```

5.

```
<HTML>
<BODY>
Opening a new window. . .
<SCRIPT LANGUAGE="JavaScript">
<!--
 var i = 10, id, w
 w = window.open("", "", "height=100,width=200")
 w.document.write("Shutting down in " + i + " seconds")
 w.document.close()
 showtime()
   //call function
 function showtime()
 {
   status = i
   id = setTimeout("showtime()", 1000)
   i--

   if (i == 0)
   {
     clearTimeout(id)
     w.close()
   }
```

```
 }
//-->
</SCRIPT>
Done!
</BODY>
</HTML>
```

6. It will loop through the properties (Netscape Navigator) and events (Internet Explorer) of the form object. Inside the with block, forms[0] is a shorthand for window.document.forms[0] and write is a shorthand for window.document.write.

7. It will write centered "Hello" in red text to a page with yellow background. fgColor, bgColor, and write are abbreviated because of the with statement.

8.

```
<HTML>
<BODY>
<SCRIPT LANGUAGE="JavaScript">
<!--
 var x = ""
 for (i = 10; i <= 30; i++)
 {
   x += i + "\t"          //add decimal & tab
   x += i.toString(2) + "\t"  //add binary
   x += i.toString(8) + "\t"  //octal
   x += i.toString(16) + "\t" //hex
   x += "\n"              //add new line
 }
 document.write("<PRE>") //use mono font
 document.write(x) //output string
//-->
</SCRIPT>
</BODY>
</HTML>
```

9.

```
<HTML>
<HEAD>
<SCRIPT LANGUAGE="JavaScript">
<!--
 function calcIt(dec)
 {
   var x = ""
```

```
    dec = Number(dec)   //convert to numeric
    x += "decimal\t" + dec + "\n"       //add decimal
    x += "binary\t" + dec.toString(2) + "\n"  //add binary
    x += "octal\t" + dec.toString(8) + "\n"  //octal
    x += "hex\t" + dec.toString(16)       //hex
    alert(x)  //output string
  }
//-->
</SCRIPT>
</HEAD>
<BODY>
<FORM>
Enter a decimal number and press Enter:<BR>
<INPUT TYPE="text" onchange="calcIt(this.value)"
</FORM>
</BODY>
</HTML>
```

10.

```
<HTML>
<HEAD>
<SCRIPT LANGUAGE="JavaScript">
<!--
  var sec = 0, min = 0
  function showtime()
  {
    sec++
    if (sec >= 60) {sec = 0; min++}
    window.status = min + " min, " + sec + " seconds"
    id = setTimeout("showtime()", 1000)
  }
//-->
</SCRIPT>
</HEAD>
<BODY onload="showtime()">
</BODY>
</HTML>
```

# Index

# D



# E, F



# G, H



# I, J

# Errata

| Page, Location | Error |
|---|---|
| viii, last line | http://www.geocities... |
| **Correction:** | http://www.geocities.com/flinweb |

| Page, Location | Error |
|---|---|
| 9, line 1 | may the parent |
| **Correction:** | may be the parent |

| Page, Location | Error |
|---|---|
| 23, line 12 | illustrate |
| **Correction:** | illustrates |

| Page, Location | Error |
|---|---|
| 24, bottom half | (about saving one line) |
| **Correction:** | (You should save the entire function.) |

| Page, Location | Error |
|---|---|
| 70, line 2 from bottom | programmer |
| **Correction:** | program |

| Page, Location | Error |
|---|---|
| 78, line 12 from bottom | SELECTED |
| **Correction:** | CHECKED |

| Page, Location | Error |
|---|---|
| 120, line 6 from bottom | 1990 |
| **Correction:** | 1900 |